Why Nations Go to War

Mark P. Worrell

The United States has been involved in many wars, sometimes for noble causes like defeating Nazism, and, at other times, it has compromised its own ideals, leading to soul searching and regrets. Some wars are celebrated as glorious achievements (World War II), some are "forgotten" (Korea), and some are "ignored" (Afghanistan). The current wars in the Middle East represent a complex interplay of motivations, challenges, and threats to America's role as the world's democratic leadership. In the case of Afghanistan, we find that during the Cold War the U.S. defense and intelligence apparatus directly and indirectly created an incalculable number of radical extremists that have now turned their sights on their former benefactor. The invasion of Iraq represents a different calculus: Under the multitude of rationalizations rests a simple political-economic case of a master nation punishing a disobedient subject. In this brief book, America's relationship with war is explored with an eye toward changes in capitalism from industrialism to post-industrialism, America's involvement in the Cold War, nuclear proliferation, terrorism, torture, culture, and ideology.

Mark P. Worrell teaches Sociological Theory and courses in Politics, Religion, and Culture at the State University of New York at Cortland. Author of one previous book, *Dialectic of Solidarity: Labor, Antisemitism, and the Frankfurt School*, Professor Worrell has published widely in scholarly journals including *Telos, Rethinking Marxism, Fast Capitalism*, and *Current Perspectives in Social Theory*.

THE SOCIAL ISSUES COLLECTION™

Framing 21st Century Social Issues

The goal of this new, unique Series is to offer readable, teachable "thinking frames" on today's social problems and social issues by leading scholars. These are available for view on http://routledge.custom gateway.com/routledge-social-issues.html.

For instructors teaching a wide range of courses in the social sciences, the Routledge *Social Issues Collection* now offers the best of both worlds: originally written short texts that provide "overviews" to important social issues *as well as* teachable excerpts from larger works previously published by Routledge and other presses.

As an instructor, click to the website to view the library and decide how to build your custom anthology and which thinking frames to assign. Students can choose to receive the assigned materials in print and/or electronic formats at an affordable price.

Body Problems
Running and Living Long in a Fast-Food Society
Ben Agger

Sex, Drugs, and Death
Addressing Youth Problems in American Society
Tammy Anderson

The Stupidity Epidemic
Worrying About Students, Schools, and America's Future
Joel Best

Empire Versus Democracy
The Triumph of Corporate and Military Power
Carl Boggs

Contentious Identities
Ethnic, Religious, and Nationalist Conflicts in Today's World
Daniel Chirot

The Future of Higher Education
Dan Clawson and Max Page

Waste and Consumption
Capitalism, the Environment, and the Life of Things
Simonetta Falasca-Zamponi

Rapid Climate Change
Causes, Consequences, and Solutions
Scott G. McNall

The Problem of Emotions in Societies
Jonathan H. Turner

Outsourcing the Womb
Race, Class, and Gestational Surrogacy in a Global Market
France Winddance Twine

Changing Times for Black Professionals
Adia Harvey Wingfield

Why Nations Go to War
A Sociology of Military Conflict
Mark Worrell

Why Nations Go to War
A Sociology of Military Conflict

Mark P. Worrell
State University of New York at Cortland

 Routledge
Taylor & Francis Group

NEW YORK AND LONDON

First published 2011
by Routledge
270 Madison Avenue, New York, NY 10016

Simultaneously published in the UK
by Routledge
2 Park Square, Milton Park, Abingdon, Oxon OX14 4RN

Routledge is an imprint of the Taylor & Francis Group, an informa business

Typeset in Garamond and Gil Sans by EvS Communication Networx, Inc.

Library of Congress Cataloging in Publication Data
Worrell, Mark P.
Why nations go to war : a sociology of military conflict / Mark P. Worrell.
p. cm. — (Framing 21st century social issues)
1. War and society—United States. 2. War—Economic aspects—United States.
3. United States—History, Military. 4. War—Causes. 5. War (Philosophy)
6. Afghan War, 2001—Social aspects—United States. 7. Iraq War, 2003—Social aspects—United States. I. Title.
HM554.W67 2011
303.6'6—dc22
2010029902

ISBN13: 978-0-415-89211-7 (pbk)
ISBN13: 978-0-203-83426-8 (ebk)

Contents

Series Foreword

The world in the early 21st century is beset with problems—a troubled economy, global warming, oil spills, religious and national conflict, poverty, HIV, health problems associated with sedentary lifestyles. Virtually no nation is exempt, and everyone, even in affluent countries, feels the impact of these global issues.

Since its inception in the 19th century, sociology has been the academic discipline dedicated to analyzing social problems. It is still so today. Sociologists offer not only diagnoses; they glimpse solutions, which they then offer to policy makers and citizens who work for a better world. Sociology played a major role in the civil rights movement during the 1960s in helping us to understand racial inequalities and prejudice, and it can play a major role today as we grapple with old and new issues.

This series builds on the giants of sociology, such as Weber, Durkheim, Marx, Parsons, Mills. It uses their frames, and newer ones, to focus on particular issues of contemporary concern. These books are about the nuts and bolts of social problems, but they are equally about the frames through which we analyze these problems. It is clear by now that there is no single correct way to view the world, but only paradigms, models, which function as lenses through which we peer. For example, in analyzing oil spills and environmental pollution, we can use a frame that views such outcomes as unfortunate results of a reasonable effort to harvest fossil fuels. "Drill, baby, drill" sometimes involves certain costs as pipelines rupture and oil spews forth. Or we could analyze these environmental crises as inevitable outcomes of our effort to dominate nature in the interest of profit. The first frame would solve oil spills with better environmental protection measures and clean-ups, while the second frame would attempt to prevent them altogether, perhaps shifting away from the use of petroleum and natural gas and toward alternative energies that are "green."

These books introduce various frames such as these for viewing social problems. They also highlight debates between social scientists who frame problems differently. The books suggest solutions, both on the macro and micro levels. That is, they suggest what new policies might entail, and they also identify ways in which people, from the ground level, can work toward a better world, changing themselves and their lives and families and providing models of change for others.

Readers do not need an extensive background in academic sociology to benefit from these books. Each book is student-friendly in that we provide glossaries of terms for the uninitiated that are keyed to bolded terms in the text. Each chapter ends with questions for further thought and discussion. The level of each book is accessible to undergraduate students, even as these books offer sophisticated and innovative analyses.

Mark Worrell explores a subject usually neglected by sociologists—war. He asks why we go to war when reason fails, and his answer is grounded in his analysis of the U.S. involvement in Iraq and Afghanistan. These are, of course, contemporary issues that dominate the headlines. Worrell traces Middle East conflict to the Ottoman Empire, providing much-needed historical background. And he considers carefully why the U.S. has a strategic interest in Afghanistan, especially in light of its relationship to the bordering nation of Pakistan. He offers a sociology of military conflict that raises important questions about our role in nation building, especially in the difficult decade since 9/11. Can we simultaneously win the hearts and minds of foreign people while fighting a war on their homeland? Should we try to make the world safe for democracy or democracy safe for the world? Worrell considers these timely questions.

Preface

This book places American military involvement in Iraq and Afghanistan within a larger historical and political-economic context from the collapse of the Ottoman Empire and the aftermath of World War I up to 2010. Of special importance is how Iraq attempted to control its national petroleum resources and how a rising tide of Arab disobedience in the 1970s led to a confrontation between the U.S. and Iraq in the early 1990s and, finally, the invasion of 2003. The war in Afghanistan represents a related but separate logic of dealing with the unintended consequences of the Cold War struggle with the Soviet Union. Afghanistan itself has little to offer the United States except for its strategic role with regard to what amounts to a paradoxical war with Pakistan—a supposed ally of the U.S. that funds and supports terrorists while accepting American weapons and cash to fight terrorists. How will current and future military operations be funded on the backs of a shrinking middle-class tax base, stagnant wages, disinvestments in domestic infrastructure, and risky financial speculations? The capitalist system in Western industrialized nations underwent dramatic transformations from about 1970 onward that have made warfare more problematic and, at the same time, more probable. Austere economic conditions breed authoritarian and reactionary politics and policies. Through control of corporate-owned mass media and the reduction of "press" and "communication" to propaganda functions, the state demands not only more in economic givebacks but also more loyalty and unquestioned obedience in an environment of increased emphasis on security and secrecy. The United States is a nation torn between the ideals of peace, freedom, and democracy but which also venerates strength and solving problems through the use of force. Will ballots prevail over bullets, or will the U.S. lose its role as the democratic leader of the world?

1: Introduction

‿‿✶‿‿

War is sustained armed conflict between societies resulting in large-scale loss of life or extreme material destruction. Engaging in war either directly or indirectly though a proxy is one of the principal means through which a society, **status group**, political party, or social class, projects force for the purpose of increasing economic, political, or geographic strength, weakening a rival, or pacifying some real or perceived threat. A civil war is defined as this kind of conflict occurring between two or more factions within a given society. The boundaries between external and internal warfare are fuzzy as participants in a civil war may receive assistance from outside supporters and may in fact fight primarily for the benefit of some external agent. Prior to the advent of the modern nation state and the cultivation of nationalist sentiments, the distinction between war and civil war were fairly indistinguishable (Johnson 1934: 335).

While nothing would seem more deliberate and calculated as the decision to go to war, there have been cases where societies find themselves at war for mysterious reasons. The U.S. invasion of Iraq is a good example of citizens being told many different stories, none of which turned out to have any bearing at all on the actual decision to fight. In other cases even the decision-makers themselves act on erroneous assumptions. In the 1850s, the mechanisms that led to the Crimean War "were so murky that after its conclusion the government of one of the principal combatants, Great Britain, appointed a commission to determine what, in fact, it had been all about" (Gelvin 2008: 176).

As an endemic, organized, and documented historical fact, war is a problem that has vexed humanity since about the time dynastic city-states ruled the Middle East (what we might think of as the first "war" occurred roughly 5,000 years ago near Basra in what is today Iraq), with less defined forms of armed conflict over material surpluses stretching back to the Neolithic Period, though there is no clear evidence that anything like routine armed conflict existed until the late Neolithic Period or perhaps around the time of the first copper or bronze tools (Hamblin 2006: 15; Keen 1986: 16).

Today, there are, at any given moment around the world, dozens of conflicts and full-blown wars being waged. In 2009, the Heidelberg Institute for International Conflict Research documented "31 conflicts fought out with the use of massive violence" (2009: 1), with seven falling under the more serious category of war. In all, the Heidelberg Institute counted 365 violent and non-violent conflicts worldwide in 2009 (2009: 1). The United States is directly or indirectly involved in many of these conflicts.

American troops have been involved in roughly 130 different conflicts since its War of Independence and indirectly involved in hundreds of other miscellaneous armed encounters around the world; on average, American forces are deployed to theaters of conflict every year or two. On top of actual fighting, American troops have also been involved in famous and politically decisive "battles" that, as it turned out, never even took place (e.g., the Gulf of Tonkin incident that drew the U.S. into defeat in Vietnam). Since 1939 Americans have experienced a continuous cycle of preparing for war, fighting, withdrawal, and rearming for the next fight and if current trends are any indication it appears that the oscillations between war and peace have given way to continuous warfare.

With the end of the Cold War in 1991 the United States emerged as the sole remaining superpower. As Samir Amin says, the U.S. is becoming the "military master of the world" (1994: 91). Given the predominant role of the U.S. in the contemporary global system of war, this book will focus on the United States, with respect to both the contemporary Middle East as well as some general and historical aspects. While the U.S. is not an old society it ranks high among the most significant war-makers in history and, in the 21st century, the United States stands unrivaled in its military prowess.

In this book I will touch upon some economic, political, cultural, and ideological functions of war with an emphasis on imperialism and capitalism. Given the brevity of this book many important aspects must, regrettably, be either completely neglected or only briefly mentioned but I hope it offers enough for students to get started.

II: The Wars in Iraq and Afghanistan

~~~~~

The U.S. and coalition invasion of Iraq and the war in Afghanistan have to be grasped within the backdrop of the creation of the modern Middle East by European powers after World War I. In addition to the simple issue of access to energy sources the role of state "police" actions and the enforcement of global discipline within the American **imperial** system is examined as well as the legacy of the Cold War in determining the nature of the war in Afghanistan. War as a wasteful enterprise and the costs of the current Middle Eastern wars are highlighted, as are the problems of nuclear weapons and torture.

The Collapse of the Ottoman Empire and World War I

Many reasons were given for the invasion of Iraq by America and its "coalition of the willing." Initially the world was told that the Iraqi regime was directly linked to the terrorist attacks on 9/11. When that connection proved to be a fantasy the claim was made that the Iraqi regime possessed weapons of mass destruction (WMD). When that line failed to pan out the rationale shifted to the "liberation" of the Iraqi people from a ruthless despot, and so on. Like finding a crime to fit the punishment, the Bush administration was bent on finding a reason, *any* reason, that might seem plausible, to legitimate what it had already decided to do: Engage in a preemptive attack on another country that did not represent a direct threat to national security. Why? Critics of the war in Iraq identified a number of reasons why the Bush administration was so gung-ho to invade: Motives ranging from personal revenge, the defense of Israel, access to cheap oil, and nebulous geopolitical strategies, and so forth.

When we step back from all the bewildering and accidental details a few important features stand out apart from relatively simple issues such as access and control over natural resources like oil. Petroleum energy is undoubtedly central to any explanation, but "oil" has to be framed within the broader context of international trade, imperial **hegemony**, global discipline, and questions of state autonomy and dependency. For now, though, we will briefly explore the origins of the modern Middle East as an outcome of World War I, and then examine the relationship between oil and the international order of political command and wealth accumulation.

Suffering defeat at Vienna in 1683, the Ottoman Empire (Turkey) began a two-century decline in political and military power. By the end of the 19th century a "perfect storm" of economic, military, and nationalistic forces were unleashed that would ultimately set the stage for World War I, the horrifying conflagration that was supposed not only to end quickly, but also to mark the end of all future wars. Within this backdrop of long-range Ottoman contraction Germany defeated the French during the Franco-Prussian War (1870–71) and welded itself into an empire that "clearly altered the distribution of power within Europe and ushered in a new international order" (Henig 1993: 3). Germany's subsequent and dramatic economic and military development from 1871 to 1914 placed it in the role of the dominant European power and, in the process, unnerved and destabilized the remainder of Europe—setting into motion a tremendous arms race and modernization of military forces. By 1907 Europe was divided between two determined power constellations: the "Triple Alliance" (Germany, Italy, and Austria–Hungary) and the "Triple Entente" (Russia, England, and France). The other decisive element in the run-up to war was emerging nationalist aspirations in the Balkans. No longer held down by Ottoman rule, the dreams of a resurgent Serbian nation took hold in opposition to the Austro–Hungarians, who had no intention of relinquishing portions of their empire. After promising support to Austria, it all came down to the Germans: "They could work to localize the conflict and to force restraint on Austria–Hungary and on Russia, or they could promise full support to their Austrian ally and run the risk of a general war" (Henig 1993: 23).

Germany felt trapped between Russia and France, that it was thwarted at every turn by the countermeasures of other European powers, and that its own internal pressures (growing worker radicalism and civil and economic unrest) put it on the fateful course for full-scale war. In the first few days of August 1914 all the major European powers except for Italy were at war (at the outbreak of war, the "Triple Alliance" that included Italy was transformed into an alliance of Germany and Austria–Hungary, the so-called "Central Powers," with the addition of the Ottomans who joined the fight in October).

The consequences of World War I were monumental for European nations but even more so for the areas once under the control of the Ottomans. The resulting political vacuum led to the victors carving up the massive landscape of the old Empire into a new and bewildering array of political and national boundaries.

Iraq

At the conclusion of World War I the European powers divided up what had been parts of the Ottoman Empire. France received what is today Syria and Lebanon, and the British received Israel, the Occupied Territory, Jordan, and Iraq. Iraq was "created" when the former Ottoman provinces of Baghdad, Mosul, and Basra were artificially stitched together (Gelvin 2008: 181–82). This dividing up the spoils of war by the Europeans is known as the "mandates system."

Article 22 of the League of Nations charter (the League was the precursor to the United Nations) established this mandates system and declared:

> there should be applied the principle that the well-being and development of such peoples form a sacred trust of civilization and that securities for the performance of that trust should be embodied in the covenant. The best method of giving practical effect to this principle should be entrusted to advanced nations who by reason of their resources, their experience, or their geographical position can best undertake this responsibility.
>
> (in Gelvin 2008: 180)

As Gelvin concludes, "the mandates system was little more than thinly disguised imperialism" (2008: 181).

Britain ruled over Iraq until it became obvious that their artificial construct exacerbated religious and ethnic tensions between groups and that maintaining order would be difficult and prohibitively expensive (Cleveland and Bunton 2009: 204–11; Gelvin 2008: 184). Iraq was granted formal independence in 1932; however, it remained a British client state during the rule of the Hashemite Monarchy from 1932 to 1958 until the Revolutionary Command Council (RCC) and the so-called Free Officers overthrew this British-friendly monarchy in a military coup d'état in 1958. The newly created Iraqi Republic was governed by a series of dictators that held power through a combination of rewards and violence (patronage).

After the 1967 Israeli war, Iraq cut ties with the United States and Great Britain and drew closer to the Soviet Union and France. The relationship between Iraq and the USSR was strengthened further in 1969 when the Soviets agreed to help develop Iraq's oil resources. In 1972 the Iraq Petroleum Company (a consortium of Western oil companies) was nationalized, eliminating "the last—and crucially important—element of foreign control from Iraq's national life" (Tripp 2007: 200), and Iraq and the Soviets signed a treaty that guaranteed sales of oil in the face of expected retaliatory embargos. The 1973 Arab–Israeli war resulted in spiking oil prices creating "unimaginable wealth in the hands of the small circle of men who controlled the Iraqi state, providing them with a means of patronage that far exceeded anything available to their predecessors" (Tripp 2007: 200). From the standpoint of Cold War America the picture was bleak—a wealthy, autonomous oil-producer friendly to, and receiving military aid from, the Soviet Union. Of course, Iraq was just one such nation.

The Organization of the Petroleum Exporting Countries (OPEC) withheld oil from the U.S. as punishment for its support of Israel in the 1973 war and then "took control of oil pricing away from the oil companies and, within a few months, quadrupled the price" (Isbister 2001: 175). OPEC hiked oil prices again in 1979, sending economic and political shockwaves through wealthy core nations:

A group of third world countries had finally succeeded in turning the tables on the rich countries. Rather than seeing their own countries sucked dry by low-priced exports that went to fuel Western industrialization, the OPEC countries were now bleeding the developed countries, showing that their former masters were vulnerable, that their prosperity depended on the resources and the cooperation of the oil exporters.

(Isbister 2001: 175)

Saddam Hussein was emerging as the most powerful person in Iraq within this new framework of rising OPEC power and Arab disobedience. His rise to power occurred during the presidency of Ahmad Hasan al-Bakr. Hussein eventually came to dominate the state security institutions and the Ba'th Party organization. "This gave him an unparalleled grasp of the administration and from here he made inroads into the officer corps, establishing his own client networks ... to whom he opened up the possibilities of enrichment and promotion if they adhered to his cause" (Tripp 2007: 207). From his position of growing power and influence, Hussein came to control Iraq's oil policies and revenue streams. Using the crisis of the Iranian Revolution and the fear of religious unrest in Iraq, Saddam Hussein seized control of the state from al-Bakr and had himself sworn in as president in July of 1979.

The long war with Iran during the 1980s (originally conceived by Hussein as a "limited war" to enhance Iraq's regional power) represents a curious turn of fortunes for Iraq. It found itself being supported financially and militarily by the Soviets *and* the United States and Britain. Suddenly, both the East and the West were on the side of Iraq. Why? Because "an Iranian military victory would radically destabilize the Middle East as a whole in a way that would be to the advantage of 'neither East nor West'" (Tripp 2007: 231). Moreover, the devastating war between Iraq and Iran represented an opportunity for 'the West' to get its hooks back into Iraq, ensnaring it in a web of debt and austerity measures designed to break state control over the economy and reestablish a steady flow of **capital** to the U.S. and Great Britain. Money and arms flowing into Iraq meant huge debts to be repaid later, and with lots of conditions attached.

Prolonging the war was phenomenally expensive. Iraq received massive external financial support from the Gulf states, and assistance through loan programs from the US. The White House and State Department pressured the Export–Import Bank to provide Iraq with financing, to enhance its credit standing and enable it to obtain loans from other international financial institutions. The US Agriculture Department provided taxpayer-guaranteed loans for purchases of American commodities, to the satisfaction of US grain exporters.

(Battle 2003)

The metaphor of a vampire sucking the life out of its victim is not misplaced with respect to the U.S., transnational capital, and Iraq. With this in mind, the Iraqi invasion of Kuwait in 1990 is comprehensible: If Kuwait could be taken by military force it could be "exchanged for substantial concessions. These would alleviate Iraq's financial position, greatly enhance Saddam Hussein's authority and establish Iraq as both the dominant power in the Gulf and a leader in the oil market" (Tripp 2007: 243). The Iraqis easily overwhelmed Kuwait but the gamble backfired in 2001 when the U.S. military crushed the Iraqi forces in the "First Gulf War"—basically, a $60 billion live-fire exercise, a campaign that was so effortless it was like shooting fish in a barrel. Far from reaping a concession, Iraq was subjected to years of United Nations sanctions and military containment.

The idea behind containment during the 1990s was to literally keep Iraq in a state of suspended animation, starving the nation to the point of death, and hopefully triggering a coup that would set in place a new regime that would be amenable to U.S. demands. That hope never materialized and, quite to the contrary, Iraq found allies in China, Europe, and in the Gulf region. To alleviate the suffering of the Iraqi people, the UN set in place an "oil for food" exchange system that unintentionally put Iraq back on the road to political and economic health.

> The economic activity these revenues generated and the widening scope of its imports made Iraq once again a hub of regional trade ... . Companies and countries which had hitherto been wary of re-entering the Iraqi market could not pass up the opportunities and inducements offered by an Iraqi government eager to encourage its commercial re-integration into the world economic system.
>
> (Tripp 2007: 268)

Iraq's success in the face of western hostility meant its doom. By 1998 the U.S. made up its mind to destroy the Hussein regime once and for all: "the fact that Saddam Hussein not only remained in power but thumbed his nose at the sanctions imposed by the international community after the war [1991] made a mockery of America's claim to dominance of global affairs" (Gelvin 2008: 269). If it could not indirectly control Iraq then the only solution was direct control and remaking the country in the image that Washington desired. The invasion of Iraq in 2003 had nothing to do with anything other than the long-standing problem of unfettered dominance and exploitation of Iraq and its resources. In a sense, the foundations for the invasion were established in 1972 when that country took control of its own oil industry—asserting authority over one's own resources or thumbing your nose at Western powers often leads to war (Gelvin 2008: 261): When Egyptian President Nasser nationalized the Suez Canal in 1956, for example, it led to swift military reaction on the part of Israel, Britain, and France (the Suez War); when the democratically elected Iranian Prime Minister, Mohammad Mossadegh, nationalized his country's oil industry the United

States organized a coup d'état in 1953 (Harvey 2003: 20) and oversaw a puppet dictator more obedient to U.S. wishes until the 1979 Islamic revolution.

There's no denying that Hussein was a ruthless dictator, a psychopathic villain, and a mass murderer. But "In spite of everything, Saddam's dictatorship did take the country into industrial, technological, and military modernization unparalleled in the modern Arab world. In 1990, the destruction of Iraq was decreed for this crime" (Amin 1994: 111).

For most Westerners "Iraq" conjures images of an ancient, ragged, war-torn, quasi-primitive outcast from the modern world system. But if Iraq (like some other "backwards" countries) appears to be defectively archaic it is not because the nation has stubbornly refused to get with the modernization program. On the contrary, Iraq is defective *because* it has been fully incorporated into the modern global system of capital accumulation. As Zizek says,

> "backwardness" and apparent "regressions" from the modernization model are "the very result of their integration into the global market and concomitant political struggles—suffice it to recall cases like Congo or Afghanistan. In other words, pre-modern sub-states are not atavistic remainders, but rather integral parts of the "postmodern" global constellation.

> (2010: 172)

Since 2003, tens of billions of dollars have flowed into Iraq in the form of loans and assistance—some of the funds are to be repaid with other streams of revenue serving as giveaways to corporations engaged in reconstruction, which amounts to a transfer of wealth from U.S. taxpayers to multinational corporations such as Halliburton, Bechtel, etc. Since February 2010 the International Monetary Fund (IMF) and the World Bank have been dumping additional billions on Iraq in the form of loans that will ensure the perpetual dependency of Iraq and mind-numbing hardships ("austerity") for its surviving population. And, rest assured, Iraqi oil resources are once again under the control of Western petroleum corporations. The fate of Iraq is just one story in a pattern of imperial domination that has played out around the globe. As Ernest Mandel argues, "the capitalist world economy is an *articulated system of capitalist, semi-capitalist and pre-capitalist relations of production linked to each other by capitalist relations of exchange and dominated by the capitalist world market*" (1975: 48–49—emphasis in original). This global system of capital accumulation is known as "dependent accumulation" (Frank 1979) where labor-rich but low-priced commodity exports (e.g., oil, agricultural crops, minerals) are exchanged for low-value but high-priced consumer imports (Mandel 1975: 53, 72–73).

Basically, dependent accumulation amounts to the conversion of a nation or even an entire region into a raw material exporter, the annihilation of its base of self-subsistence, and importer of consumer goods necessary for the continuation of its export economy. The consequence is the exchange of unequal values (Frank 1979: 21–22). The more the dependent country exports the faster and deeper it digs its own grave. Uneven development of nations rests on this fundamental logic of imbalanced international trade between wealthy core ("metropolitan") nations and impoverished ("peripheral") countries (Frank 1979: 172). Export specialization in things like oil or bananas (what is sometimes, erroneously, referred to as a nation's "competitive advantage") creates and recreates relations of dependency and servitude (Wolf 1982: 313). So, in reality, a nation's "advantage" is really its undoing except for a minority **power elite** that profits greatly from cooperation with the U.S. and big firms in keeping the rest of the population down.

To the extent that a nation sets out to rectify the imbalance (e.g., Iraq nationalizing its own oil industry) the imperial core resorts to sanctions and military force to restore dominance. That Iraq is now under direct U.S. occupation seals its fate. Iraq has been liberated from a dictatorial tyrant but the Iraqi people have gained a new master. Deprived of control over its own resources, the Iraqi people will have to rely on the benevolence of their new administrators. Oil is, undeniably, an important reason why the U.S. invaded. On the eve of invasion President Bush addressed the Iraqi people: "all Iraqi military and civilian personnel should listen carefully to this warning. In any conflict, your fate will depend on your action. Do not destroy oil wells, a source of wealth that belongs to the Iraqi people."

But oil is not the whole story. Clearly, the decision to remove Hussein and his clique by force was also a case of *disciplining* a disobedient state actor and, in the process, disciplining other similarly situated nations and their allies in the world system. As Hardt and Negri claim, the war in Iraq was also an indirect attack on Europe: "not only in the political way it was conducted but also in the threat to European industry posed by U.S. control of Iraqi energy resources." The strategy of identifying an "Axis of Evil" (Iraq, Iran, North Korea) and attacking Iraq served the "function of challenging and weakening the primary strategic competitors [Europe, Russia, and China] that threaten US unilateral control" (2004: 317). Indeed, we can see in the American "solution" to Iraq a reaction to "the faint outlines of a Eurasian power bloc" of France, Germany, Russia, China under development. "The US invasion of Iraq then takes on an even broader meaning. Not only does it constitute an attempt to control the global oil spigot and hence the global economy through domination over the Middle East. It also constitutes a powerful U.S. military bridgehead on the Eurasian land mass" (Harvey 2003: 85).

Afghanistan

Afghanistan is blessed with natural resources such as lithium, iron, gold, copper, and cobalt (recently estimated at nearly a trillion dollars' worth) as well as gas, coal, and some oil, but the U.S. and its allies are not in Afghanistan for the purpose of extracting these resources. Presently, there is nothing by way of infrastructure to support mining and the social organization of the country is unsuited to take advantage of large-scale mining or other industrial activities. Trying to exploit Afghanistan's locked-up natural wealth would probably be more trouble than it is worth, at least in the foreseeable future (see Riechmann and Flaherty 2010). The importance of Afghanistan for the United States is its *geographic* location and how its boundaries and proximities play into national security and the energy resources of Central Asia overall.

> For few countries in the world is it more true that geography determines history, politics and the nature of a people. Afghanistan's geo-strategic location on the crossroads between Iran, the Arabian Sea and India and between Central Asia and South Asia has given its territory and mountain passes a significance since the earliest Aryan invasions 6,000 years ago.
>
> (Rashid 2000: 7)

Ostensibly, the U.S. is operating in Afghanistan in an effort to locate and capture **Osama bin Laden**, defeat **al Qaeda**, and curb the **Taliban**. What most Americans know about jihadi extremist groups is that they are the mortal enemies of the United States. True, they are not our friends and they are extremely dangerous, but what most people do not know is that many if not most jihadi groups are the creations "of Pakistani and Western intelligence outfits, born in the 1980s when General Zia was in power and waging the West's war against godless Russians, who were then occupying Afghanistan. It was then that state patronage of Islamist groups began" (Ali 2008: 12; Rashid 2000: 19). Not only are U.S. forces battling al Qaeda but also its national host, our supposed ally, the Pakistani army. Not for the first time has the U.S. been forced to hunt down its own monstrous creations. Some background is in order.

In the 19th and early 20th centuries, Great Britain poured vast sums of money, weapons, and various other resources into Afghanistan in support of a proxy government that could function as a buffer, protecting its colonial holdings in India from Russian incursions. In 1919 Afghanistan was granted formal independence and from the mid-1950s to 1978 the country came under the hegemony of the Soviet Union. An internal power grab by Marxist military officers in 1978 resulted in a coup that toppled the government; the quarreling political factions that orchestrated the coup were unable to solidify command and the religious leaders of Afghanistan, the mullahs, declared a holy war (jihad) against the various communist forces, triggering a Soviet invasion and occupation of the country from the end of 1979 to 1989. Afghanistan became a central battlefield in the Cold War between the U.S. and the USSR. The United States and other nations with energy interests in Central Asia backed the Islamic fundamentalist forces, known as the Mujaheddin, against the Soviet Union. Once the Soviets withdrew in 1989 the country disintegrated into a multitude of warring factions ruled by warlords, drug cartels, and other criminal bands. So long as chaos reined, Afghanistan represented a problem for international trade and vital trade routes connecting various Asian commercial hubs as well as a refugee problem for Pakistan (Rashid 2000).

To understand the "problem" of Afghanistan just look at a map of the country. It is bordered by Pakistan, Iran, three central Asian republics that were formerly a part of the Soviet system and still more or less Russian proxies (Turkmenistan, Uzbekistan, and Tajikistan), and China (it connects with Afghanistan along a tiny mountain pass in the Hindu Kush).

And even though they are not physically in contact, Russia, India, Saudi Arabia, Turkey, and the United States all have interests in Afghanistan as well. India has a problem with Pakistan; China has a problem with India; Russia has a problem with China; they all have problems with the U.S.; it goes on and on. On top of that, southern Afghanistan has been the imagined route of oil and gas pipelines from Turkmenistan to the Arabian Sea (Rashid 2009: 15).

After nine years of conventional military operations and new "counterinsurgency" strategies, the U.S. is apparently no closer to winning in Afghanistan that it was when it began; Leon Panetta, the director of the Central Intelligence Agency (CIA), could only muster a limp "making progress" assessment (June 2010) with regard to U.S. efforts, while noting that "It's harder, it's slower than I think anyone anticipated." Of course, it does not help that the U.S. is not even trying to support the Afghan government, preferring instead to dump money on petty warlords—a recent report entitled "Warlord, Inc." by the Subcommittee on National Security and Foreign Affairs (U.S. House of Representatives) found that the Defense Department's outsourcing of logistics to local contractors in Afghanistan "had significant unintended consequences. The HNT [Host Nation Trucking] contract fuels warlordism, extortion, and corruption, and it may be a significant source of funding for insurgents" (Tierney 2010: 2). So, what is really going on in Afghanistan?

The real agenda for the U.S. forces is actually Pakistan. After 9/11 Pakistan reemerged as a major but unreliable ally of the U.S. While accepting over $10 billion dollars from the United States between 2002 and 2007 to help defeat terrorism, it was actually supporting, training, and arming terrorists. Why? Because Pakistan is really only interested in undermining India. Pakistan is a mass producer of violent religious fanatics and anti-U.S. terrorists (Zakaria 2010) because they are used as human weapons to keep India off balance in the region. Helping to prop up the Taliban and al Qaeda in Afghanistan was seen as a protective measure against Indian power—as was supporting insurgents in Kashmir that nearly dragged the two countries into multiple, large-scale wars. The Taliban is so connected to the Pakistani army that it might as well be seen as a virtual wing of their national security apparatus. Pakistani military and intelligence units also support the Taliban because they hope to one day occupy and rule Afghanistan, once the U.S. and NATO have decamped (Ali 2008: 26). As of the summer of 2010, nothing much changed between the U.S. and Pakistan: money and weapons flow into Islamabad, the Pakistanis put on another performance of their long-running theatrical production "Rounding up Some Terrorists," and after getting praised by Washington for their cooperation and rewarded with more money and weapons, the Pakistanis go back to supporting the same terrorists—what one observer called the Pakistani "Catch and Release" program.

After 2007, the U.S. adopted a more nuanced approach to Pakistan by increasing recognition and cooperation with India—to pressure Pakistan (by feeding its paranoia) to comply more fully with U.S. demands and also because India will be needed in the future to contain China in a new cold war between the U.S. and a China/Eurasian bloc. The other main reason the U.S. is fighting Pakistan in Afghanistan is because Pakistan has a nuclear weapons capability and the idea of terrorists getting their hands on the trigger of Armageddon is truly horrifying. The possibility of Pakistan aiding others with regard to nuclear capability is not just fanciful speculation; Pakistan has already provided materials, instruments, and technical help to Iran, North Korea, and Libya (Rashid 2009: 287–89). Victory in the Middle East may well simply equate with preventing the detonation of one or more nuclear warheads.

Casualties and Costs: An Orgy of Waste and Destruction

As of May 14, 2010, the U.S. Department of Defense (DoD) reported that 4,401 troops and civilian employees of the DoD had been killed in Iraq ("Operation Iraqi Freedom") with an additional 1,058 killed in Afghanistan ("Operation Enduring Freedom"), giving a total of nearly 5,500. The number of troops wounded in both theaters of operation over the same timeframe totaled 37,641 according to the official DoD reports. But in his February 4, 2010 testimony before the House Committee on Veterans' Affairs, Paul Sullivan, the Executive Director of Veterans for Common Sense (VCS) charged that these official DoD figures are grossly inaccurate. Requesting documents through the Freedom of Information (FoI) Act, the VCS obtained data from the Veterans Administration indicating that the VA provided medical care to more than 508,000 wounded, sick, or ill veteran patients of the wars in Iraq and Afghanistan and that more than 9,000 patients are added to the rolls every month.

Civilian casualties in the Middle East are much more difficult to calculate. The World Health Organization and *The New England Journal of Medicine* estimated that 151,000 Iraqi civilians had been killed in hostilities between March 2003 and June 2006 (Iraq Family Health Survey Study Group 2008). The use of unmanned drones (Predator and Reaper models) is especially problematic. In Afghanistan and Pakistan mass carnage is being unleashed on the local population. Trying to kill the head of

Taliban forces in Pakistan, Baitulla Mehsud, took the CIA 16 attempts and more than a year before they bagged their target.

> During this hunt, between two hundred and seven and three hundred and twenty-one additional people were killed, depending on which news accounts you rely upon. It's all but impossible to get a complete picture of whom the CIA killed during this campaign.
>
> (Mayer 2009).

During a February 2010 drone attack in Uruzgan more than 30 innocent civilians were killed when their vehicles were mistaken for an insurgent convoy:

> In the Uruzgan incident, coalition aircraft attacked three vehicles with more than 30 civilians who were mistaken for insurgents, according to U.S. Army Maj. Gen. Timothy McHale, who reviewed the incident. The Predator crew "ignored or downplayed" intelligence that the "convoy was anything other than an attacking force," the report said. The tragedy "was compounded by a failure of the commands involved to timely report the incident," it said. "The strike occurred because the ground force commander lacked a clear understanding of who was in the vehicles, the location, direction of travel and the likely course of action of the vehicles," he said. "This lack of understanding resulted from poorly functioning command posts … which failed to provide the ground force commander with the evidence and analysis that the vehicles were not a hostile threat and the inaccurate and unprofessional reporting of the Predator crew operating out of Creech [Air Force Base in] Nevada which deprived the ground force commander of vital information," McHale said in his report.
>
> (CNN 2010)

If we are concerned with "winning hearts and minds" and making friends in the world, the use of covert programs of indiscriminate killing are counterproductive. Even if we don't care if the wife, best friend, and some bodyguards of a terrorist are killed in one of these attacks, the issue is far more complicated. It is not uncommon for drone attacks to not only kill the "wrong guy" but our allies and supporters as well:

> The first two CIA air strikes of the Obama Administration took place on the morning of January 23rd—the President's third day in office. Within hours, it was clear that the morning's bombings, in Pakistan, had killed an estimated twenty people. In one strike, four Arabs, all likely affiliated with al Qaeda, died. But in the second strike a drone targeted the wrong house, hitting the residence of a pro-government tribal leader six miles outside the town of Wana, in South Waziristan.

The blast killed the tribal leader's entire family, including three children, one of them five years old. In keeping with U.S. policy, there was no official acknowledgment of either strike.

(Mayer 2009)

Another disturbing aspect of drone attacks is that the practice of killing off suspected terrorist leaders in such a fashion violates U.S. law prohibiting state-sponsored assassinations—the U.S. officially denounced the Israelis for doing the same thing before 9/11. Weirdly, it is not just the military that is doing the killing but also the Central Intelligence Agency (they have their own drone planes) and private contractors (e.g., Blackwater/Xe Services) who run drone programs as well (Mayer 2009). So we have a situation where large numbers of assassinations are being carried out and there is no accountability. We do not know who is doing the shooting or who is authorizing the killings—everything is secret.

On top of these political "costs" are the actual, monetary costs that the current wars are inflicting upon American taxpayers. According to the Congressional Budget Office, the U.S. has spent $345 billion in support of operations in Afghanistan and $708 billion in Iraq. So far, then, since 2001, the U.S. has spent a little over $1 trillion in Iraq and Afghanistan—it costs roughly $500,000 to support a "pair of boots on the ground for one year." After post-combat expenses are taken into consideration, e.g., benefits and healthcare, the cost may reach as high as $1 million per veteran.

War is incredibly expensive and wasteful in ways that set it apart from the festivities of the modern world. As Caillois said, it "does not correspond in the least to prodigality of lavish ceremonial expenditures and religious sacrifices; modern wars mechanically fleece the public of its wealth, the benefit of which flows upward into the accounts of corporations and elites."

There are no longer mountains of food or lakes of drink, for war is concerned with an entirely different kind of consumption. Thousands of tons of projectiles are used each day. Arsenals are emptied as rapidly as granaries. Just as all disposable foods are amassed for the festival, so loans, levies, and requisitions drain the varied riches of a country and throw them into the abyss of war, which absorbs them without ever being amassed.... The cost of several hours' hostilities represents such a considerable sum that one could believe it possible to put an end to the misery of the whole world with it.

(Caillois 1959: 169–70)

According to the U.S. Office of Management and Budget, the U.S. Department of Defense will soak up nearly $550,000,000,000 in fiscal year 2011 (roughly a quarter of the entire federal budget). Much of those funds literally go up in smoke as a result of the massive fraud and waste built into the privatization of logistical and support functions. If war has always been costly, in the last generation war has become even more expensive due to deeper corporate integration.

It used to be that the U.S. military was more or less self-sufficient and self-contained—troops were fed by their fellow soldiers, troops washed their own clothes, troops were based in camps that military engineers constructed, the military trained their own mechanics to fix their jeeps and tanks, and they policed and investigated themselves, etc. Now, the boundaries between soldiers and corporate contractors are blurred. To fund costly high-tech weapons systems the DoD has been forced over the years to downsize by cutting payroll and outsourcing functions that used to be carried out by military personnel. The lean and mean strategy that corporations adopted in the 1980s and 1990s (hurting American workers) applied to the military as well. The irony is that the outsourced services carry a price tag ultimately far in excess of what it would have cost the military to simply do the job itself.

In 2006 there were more than 100,000 private contractors working in Iraq and the surrounding region performing functions many of which would have been performed directly by the military itself in previous wars. Just as "downsizing" has ravaged the prospects of America's workers since the 1980s, the U.S. military also underwent an ideological and organizational transformation toward a "leaner and meaner" profile that places emphasis on speed and elaborate and expensive weapons platforms and programs. Corporate America wondered: Why are taxpayers spending a couple of dollars an hour to have a low-ranking soldier shovel hash browns at a mess hall when they could be paying the "private sector" (maybe a Halliburton) thousands of dollars per month for the same services but with lower efficiency and diminished competence? And wouldn't it be great, these corporations wondered, if we couldn't just skip all that messy "free market" and "competition" mumbo jumbo and just operate like a monopoly cartel and, on top of that, charge the government whatever we want? And that is what happened.

"Sole source" contracting means that no competitive bidding process among rival firms is utilized. Halliburton, for example, received contract preferences and skirted normal, institutionalized bidding processes. It is difficult to imagine that having Halliburton's former chief executive officer, Dick Cheney, in the White House did not play a decisive role in determining the outcome of contract negotiations. Indeed, in 2005 Judicial Watch obtained communications records through the Freedom of Information Act that indicate that the awarding of contracts to Halliburton was "coordinated" through the office of the Vice President, Dick Cheney, the former CEO of the firm.

"Cost-plus" pricing is a mechanism that contractors like to use when billing the government for goods and services. It means that all their costs are paid for with a surcharge tacked on at the end that guarantees, no matter what, that a handsome profit is made at the end of the day. This is the antithesis of "free market" principles and promotes gross waste and fraud; the more money that is spent, driving up the cost of a program, the more money is netted by the firm. During the rebuilding of Iraq we witnessed a nearly unlimited number of absurd abuses and fraud. For example, rather than changing the oil or a spare tire on a new truck, contractors would sometimes blow it up then bill the U.S. for a whole new replacement vehicle. Another good example is billing the military for laundry at $100 per washer load and prohibiting troops from washing their own uniforms (Greenwald 2006). It should come as no surprise, then (this is commercial piracy after all), that many of the logistics contractors working in Iraq were not and are still not well-paid Americans "serving their country" but people from underdeveloped nations earning a couple of dollars per hour (Chatterjee 2010). While private contracting of logistics in war zones represents odious business practices, the privatization of troops is a bit more ominous.

Mercenary armies are an ancient institution. It used to be that serving in a military capacity was "an honorific privilege of propertied men" (Weber 1978: 981). But **capitalism** inexorably strips the vast majority of people of ownership of private property—making them available ("freeing them up" as it were) for employment in private industry or for service in mass armies. If there are not enough of the dispossessed available for military duty, or, as the case may be, the average level of ability on the part of the troops is insufficient, the state is forced to engage mercenaries to carry out its mission. "This process typically goes hand in hand with the general increase in material and intellectual culture" (Weber 1978: 981). Simply put, the more education and life chances a person has the less likely they are to resort to employment in the military. Talented, intelligent, and creative people do not find the lure of "total institutions" (prisons, asylums, military units, etc.) to be very appealing but the military cannot function properly if their ranks are made up entirely of disposable "bio mass." Here, we find the logic of social and class **polarization** at work in the realm of armed conflict: just like American society, the "middle" is being downsized resulting in a generic mass of semi-disciplined, low-skilled warriors populating one end of the spectrum (regular "grunt" units) with a small military elite, e.g., Marine Force Recon companies and Surveillance and Target Acquisition (STA) platoons, Navy SEAL teams, the Army's Combat Applications Group and 75th Ranger Regiment, etc., at the other end of the spectrum, with extensive training, capable of complex and exotic operations. Like the capitalist labor market in general, high skill commands high wages: The cream of the crop are now lured out of low-paying military work and into the private sector, civilian employees of private security contracting firms earning sometimes thousands of dollars per week.

Private mercenaries operate with minimal oversight and virtually no accountability to Congress or the American people. Overall, a double standard exists in the prosecution of crimes in war zones. DoD personnel are finding themselves being ordered around by civilian, corporate contract employees who are not formally part of the military chain of command. When the military police and interrogators at **Abu Ghraib** prison followed orders given to them by employees of private firms they were held responsible for their actions under the Uniform Code of Military Justice (UCMJ) and subject to court-martial, but the private employees faced, at worse, being fired, returning home, and, if they so desired, returning to Iraq as an employee of some other firm. Double standards also apply to training and qualifications of civilian employees performing jobs that used to be assigned to highly trained troops. Today is the era of the amateur.

Amateurism—a special feature of the neo-conservative movement and the Bush administration's rebuilding of Iraq—has become a normal part of state operations including warzone reconstruction and disaster relief work (e.g., Michael "Brownie" Brown's leadership of the Federal Emergency Management Agency under President Bush). Amateurism is the effect of political loyalty and loyalty is the guiding principle of a political party or administration when they know that what they are doing is either illegal or easily perceived as falling under the aura of criminal behavior. Perhaps nowhere has this idea been more evident than in the rebuilding of Iraq (Chandrasekaran 2006: 84–85), where the only qualification for an important job was loyalty to President Bush.

In place of the 6,600 required police advisers in Iraq, the administration sent one person, Bernie Kerik, former New York police commissioner, who "lacked policing experience in post-conflict situations, but the White House viewed that as an asset" (Chandrasekaran 2006: 84–86). Kerik had something better than the correct policing qualifications: he was ideologically pure.

> Men such as Kerik—committed Republicans with an accomplished career in business or government—were thought to be ideal. They were loyal and they shared the Bush administration's goal of rebuilding Iraq in an American image. With Kerik, there was a bonus: the media loved him, and the American public trusted him.
>
> (Chandrasekaran 2006: 84–85)

Kerik was later convicted on eight felony charges including tax fraud, corruption, and lying to White House officials; in February 2010 Kerik was sentenced to four years in federal prison (Dolnick 2010).

Ten "gofers" hired to perform low-level clerical tasks found their way to Iraq to help in the rebuilding efforts. Their qualifications included being the daughter of a neo-con talking head and another was "a recent graduate from an evangelical university for home-schooled children," and so on. "Because of the personnel shortage in Baghdad, six of the gofers were assigned to manage Iraq's $13 billion budget, even though they had no previous financial-management experience" (Chandrasekaran 2006: 94). The person selected to rebuild the Iraq stock market, Jay Hallen, was not only spectacularly unqualified for his job, he didn't even have a background in economics or finance aside from "a brief fling as an entrepreneur in a [Yale] campus adaptation of Dr. Seuss's *The Lorax*" (Chandrasekaran 2006: 96).

Are these the kinds of people that get sent in if the real goal is actual rebuilding? It should come as no surprise that the "rebuilding" of Iraq is not the actual goal of the U.S. A nation cannot be rebuilt if virtually its entire middle class is absent. In the aftermath of the war in Iraq almost everybody with an education, connections, money, and resources (the professionals that make up the middle class) evacuated by the millions and have not returned. All that is left is the elite and their military forces floating on top of millions of disposed peasants.

Weird Juxtapositions of Modern War

When I say that war is "weird" I mean that, like a lot of other weird social phenomena (capitalism, racism, nationalism, propaganda, and so on), war is a condition of polar extremes: The wealthiest nations pounding the poorest into the dirt; unskilled and interchangeable personnel operating the most sophisticated weaponry in history; and the simultaneous presence of the most ultra-sophisticated weaponry (thermonuclear devices) and the most primitive and barbaric practices (torture). Let's look for a moment at the issue of unskilled operators of high-tech machinery.

Innovations in the instruments of warfare mean that combatants are no longer required to possess extraordinary physical or intellectual prowess; pushing buttons and operating unmanned aircraft can be performed by the "average Joe" which means that, like the world of employment, an ever-increasing pool of candidates is made available for duty. One does not have to possess culinary training to work at a fast-food restaurant. Likewise, most combatants do not have to possess exotic or precious martial skills to succeed in battle—I personally witnessed the transformation of Midwestern farm hands into Marines in about the same amount of time it takes an undergraduate to complete one semester of college. In one sense technology has made war easier to prosecute. However, there is a contradiction built into the apparent depreciation of personal strength and the increasingly irrelevance of personal valor: "the valor of cultivated nations is characterized by the very fact, that it does not rely on the strong arm alone, but places its confidence essentially in the intelligence, the generalship, the character of its commanders" (Hegel 1956: 402). What the great philosopher was getting at is that the process of technological rationalization (e.g., the development of gunpowder that enables a "cowardly wretch" to kill the most noble warrior from a safe distance) also entails the increased reliance on reason and deliberation, not only in whether or not a war should be fought (apart from simple considerations of brute strength alone) but also regarding what kinds of weapons should or should not be used against combatants. Would it not be cheaper and easier simply to detonate a thermonuclear device over our opponent than to invade, conquer, and occupy their land for years or decades? But the fact that we possess enough power to literally obliterate the planet many times over means that we also have to reflect on what kind of people we are and what our ultimate values consist of. Perhaps the weirdest paradox of conflict in the nuclear age is the twin juxtaposition of the ultimate weapon, the nuclear warhead, and the most primitive brutality, torture.

For Hardt and Negri war becomes an "absolute" (an idea that hangs over everybody guaranteeing existential coherency but also anxiety) when weapons finally achieve the capacity to eliminate all life from the surface of the planet

> War has always involved the destruction of life, but in the twentieth century this destructive power reached the limits of the pure production of death, represented symbolically by Auschwitz and Hiroshima. The capacity of genocide and nuclear destruction touches directly on the very structure of life, corrupting it, perverting it. The sovereign power that controls such means of destruction is a form of *biopower* in this most negative and horrible sense of the term, a power that rules directly over death—the death not simply of an individual or group but of humanity itself and perhaps indeed of all being … . Biopower wields not just the power of the mass destruction of life (such as that threatened by nuclear weapons) but also *individualized* violence. When individualized in its extreme form, biopower becomes torture. Torture is today becoming an ever more generalized technique of control, and at the same time it is becoming increasingly banalized.
>
> (Hardt and Negri 2004: 18–19)

Torture and nuclear weapons, as we see here, are forms of control—specifically, the forms of controlling and disciplining the external other, defending against the external threat, reducing the other to a zero point. While the U.S. military does have a vast array of internal national functions, economic, political, and cultural, torture is typically reserved for the external enemy. In what we have seen regarding the U.S. decision to invade Iraq and the reasons for the quagmire in Afghanistan we must look to the role of the military in the affairs of capital and its march across the face of the earth. If nuclear bombs and torture represent a "weird" juxtaposition it is because we live in a world where the single most decisive force, the driving power of life itself, capitalism, is the weirdest thing of all.

DISCUSSION QUESTIONS

1. Why did the U.S. invade Iraq?
2. What did the terrorist attacks of September 11, 2001 have to do with the war in Iraq?
3. Why are U.S. troops fighting in Afghanistan?
4. How can the U.S. claim moral leadership in the world if it resorts to torturing captives?

III: The Economic Functions of War

War is a lot older than capitalism but any comprehension of modern warfare must include the role of global capitalism as a primary explanatory factor. The shift from industrial to so-called post-industrial and imperial forms of capital are elaborated upon, as are the various contradictions of capitalism as they pertain to the experience of war in the lives of everyday Americans.

The Post-Industrial Economy

During the Gilded Age (the period of American history that corresponds more or less with the end of the Civil War and a massive economic collapse on the eve of the 20th century), the economy was a volatile mixture of boom and bust cycles, the accumulation and loss of vast personal fortunes, rapid industrialization, business **monopolization**, vast influxes of immigrants to rapidly expanding cities, extreme labor unrest and class conflict, rapid changes in transportation and communications technologies, etc. The ideological cement that solidified the Gilded Age was the idea of "individualism"—a man pulled himself up by his own bootstraps and survived or failed based on his own wits, cunning, ruthlessness, brutality, and shrewd business acumen.

The Progressive Era (from around the turn of the 20th century to World War I) was a period of reform movements that set out to rectify the horrendous structural problems of industrial and monopoly capital and also transform the moral and intellectual qualities of the American working class. Perhaps most importantly, the Progressive Era centered on cleaning up political corruption and witnessed a growth in state intervention in the economy and the life of workers. Though the state did not do a lot, the widespread notion began to ferment that the state should be more active in ameliorating the deep contradictions and pathologies associated with capitalism. "Fordism" (named after Henry Ford) emerged during the Progressive Era and is usually associated with the manufacturing of the Model T automobile.

The essence of Fordism was rapid assembly-line production of standardized, low-priced products constructed from interchangeable parts, marketed toward a new class of affluent (high-wage) workers and a growing middle class of consumers who enjoyed a rising standard of living. In its earliest phases of development (from World War I to World War II) Fordism was primarily a philosophy of manufacturing, "making the whole life of the nation revolve around production. Hegemony here is born in the factory and requires for its exercise only a minute quantity of professional political and ideological intermediaries" (Gramsci 1971: 283).

In its later phases from the end of World War II to roughly 1970 Fordism was a complex of social, cultural, economic, and political institutions including an active and interventionist state and a fairly dense network of commercial and financial regulations; high levels of unionized labor and labor collaboration with capital; assembly-line manufacturing; high-wage industrial jobs; product standardization; mass consumption and consumerism; an expanding middle class; job security; legal protections and appeals systems for workers; the expansion of the post-war, post-secondary educational system that gave rise to an explosion in the white-collar professional ranks, suburbanization, gender and ethnic enfranchisement; increasing leisure time; corporate cultivation of popular monoculture; and so on (Harrison and Bluestone 1998: 84–85; Harvey 1990: 125–40). As Harvey puts it, "Postwar Fordism has to be seen … less as a mere system of mass production and more as a total way of life" (1990: 135). Central to understanding the post-war Fordist system of capital accumulation was the expanding role of the state—a role that emerged from the chaos of the Great Depression and the various New Deal initiatives enacted in an attempt to kick-start the faltering economy and save capitalism from itself. Ultimately, it was the onset of World War II and the reorientation of the U.S. economy around the looming war that would save capitalism. Perhaps more than any other event, World War II taught politicians and business leaders that war and mass destruction were helpful in sustaining long-term corporate profitability.

World War II reduced most of Europe and Japan to smoldering rubble and ash. The U.S. victory over **fascism** and the subsequent rebuilding of whole societies put America in a position of great military, political, and economic power. Most importantly, though, was the relationship between the United States and the Soviet Union. The Cold War was the decisive fact of post-World War II global power relations and it spawned numerous "hot" wars on virtually every continent as the U.S. and the USSR fought each other on foreign shores through proxies and intermediaries (Korea, Vietnam, Nicaragua, Southern Africa, Afghanistan, etc.). The business climate at the end of the 1960s and early 1970s became unbearable for corporations (Europe and Japan had fully recovered and were providing competition for U.S. firms and, as we have seen, oil-producing nations in the Middle East were challenging Western hegemony) so a corporate–conservative political revolution was mapped out such that the post-war accord between the American public (labor) and the corporate elite (capital) was scuttled. From the late 1970s (Carter administration) onward, and without the slightest deviation from any president including Obama, the state committed itself to assisting corporations in extracting the wealth of the "middle class" that had once benefited from collaboration with employers.

Whereas the state from the 1930s through the 1960s acted, more or less, as a quasi-incompetent mediator between the demands of capital and labor, the state from the

1980s onward represents, almost exclusively, the interests of capital. In a sense, we can say that the state has, in the last generation, become a police force for capital in its war against the American public and the rest of the world. For citizens of the U.S., the corporate controlled state is engaged in a massive program of transferring wealth from the middle class to the top of the socio-economic order through the dismantling of Fordist-era regulatory mechanisms and the replacement of rising wages with easy access to credit that will never be repaid, reducing Americans to a peon-like existence of perpetual bondage (Leicht and Fitzgerald 2007).

Post-Fordism (from about 1970 to now) is built upon the problems of the older regime of capital accumulation. In the post-war era, the capitalist class was forced by the state to share with those that produced the wealth through a progressive tax structure and a welfare system that protected the vulnerable from unemployment, hunger and malnutrition, and other deprivations in housing and education, etc. Essentially, the post-war era was marked by forced internal investment in the nation: wealth was injected into our highways and bridges (infrastructure), educational systems, health and human services, and so on. But the wealthy grew tired of sharing our wealth and high taxes and set out to wage a war against what they referred to as the "inflexibility" of the Fordist system—"flexibility" basically means unfettered dispossession of the working class. From 1970 onward, the wealthy elite of America began to literally devour the American public like a pack of ravenous wolves.

Capital's first lines of attack were reflected in the rise of additional unpaid labor in the form of the self-service revolution; transformations in automation and "continuous process production" (refinements in Henry Ford's assembly-line system); and an increasing reliance on women and immigrants (lower pay and increased exploitability) in the workplace (see O'Connor 1984: 113–16). Capital then set its sights on totally subordinating the federal government to its exclusive needs. The Reagan "revolution" marked the beginnings of this transformation whereby the state got "off the backs" of the wealthy and put the tax burden squarely on the backs of everyday Americans. Taxes were slashed (capital gains taxes, or, the taxes on *unearned* income are fixed at only 17 percent now); virtually every form of regulation set into place during the post-war era was eliminated or severely curtailed; organized labor was crushed; jobs were eliminated as firms outsourced production overseas; the environment was trashed; and the forced internal investments of the post-war era were reversed. Capital investments were eschewed in favor of high-stakes gambling (financial speculations) that repeatedly blew up in the face of Wall Street—forcing taxpayers to pick up the bill every time—and destructive management practices that hurt the long-term health of companies for the sake of short-term profits in the form of manipulated equities prices and fixed capital liquidation (Krier 2005). Most damaging of all, virtually the entire working class received no pay increases at all for more than 40 years. Wages went up, but not enough to keep pace with inflation. Instead of increased wages in support of a rich lifestyle, Americans relied on credit and loans that, as it turns out, they could not afford. The reason the mountain of debt could not be repaid was because the promise of good jobs with rising wages was pulled out from underneath them. The manufacturing sector was gutted, replaced by 'service' jobs. Today, youth look forward to lives without careers, toiling away for pitiful wages, wasting away in the service sector: toting and fetching, retail sales, scrubbing toilets and mopping floors, lawn mowing, flipping burgers, rent-a-cops, cleaning bed pans, telemarketing, etc.

The big area of growth in state functions was the Department of Defense (DoD) that, by now, has become *quite literally* a government unto itself. Today, the U.S. spends half of its discretionary funds on the military and as of 2008 the U.S. was spending as much money on its military as the rest of the nations of the world combined (Rashid 2009). The massive increase in Pentagon power has given a mighty swagger to the gait of top Pentagon brass and field commanders—reflected in the recent incident in which Stanley McChrystal, the commanding general over operations in Afghanistan, was forced to resign in disgrace after a profile in a now-infamous *Rolling Stone* article (June 2010) revealed the level of contempt that the DoD has for Washington politicians and diplomats (i.e., civilians).

In the face of dwindling investments in the U.S., the power elite and its subordinate state mechanism turn outward in every sense of the word: into the otherworldly realm of wild financial speculations and ill-conceived military adventures overseas on behalf of energy, defense, logistics, and aerospace firms. Today we are "tilting at windmills"—battling "Terror" around the globe, drowning the American public in *trillions* of dollars of debt that will bankrupt what remains of its entitlements and safety nets.

During the post-war period the American public was mobilized in the project to defeat socialism (including on the battlefields of Korea and Vietnam) and the exploitation of the earth's population for its own benefit and bountiful lifestyle. Since the 1970s, however, the shift to a new regime of capital accumulation has assigned a new role for the American public: To be the willing fighter against the nebulous enemy, Terror (after all, serving your country beats serving up a large order of fries) while, ironically, being economically reduced to the status of neo-peasantry (Leicht and Fitzgerald 2007). What was it that President Bush asked America to do even before the smoke of 9/11 could clear the air? Go to Disneyland. Binge on credit and when the kids want to go to college they can fund that increasingly irrelevant task on the GI Bill or loans. Serving your country, now, means assisting your multi-national corporate master to suck the life out of the family members you left behind at the mall.

My uncles fought to defeat totalitarian Japan, fascist Italy, and Nazi Germany during World War II. My father served in the Navy during the Korean War. And I was a Marine through the early and late 1980s. We all joined up because we thought that America, even if far from perfect, was worth defending and there were real things in the world that, even if we didn't understand them very well, needed to be resisted. American military and political actions have always been conditioned by economic considerations but the political and ideological enemies we faced were concretely real: Nazis actually existed and were evil; the Cuban missile crisis was a real event; the Berlin Wall really was where it appeared on a map. By contrast the new war on 'Terror' is only a virtual reality—a purely political concoction, a "rhetorical device" used by Washington to stun and subdue the American public. "*Terrorism* cannot be party to a conflict, so there can be no war against it" (Rashid 2009: xlvii).

Undeniably, there are bad and violent people in the world that have done and will continue to do harm to Americans, but the magic words "Terror" and "war on terrorism" were conjured up by politicians (both liberal and conservative) in a ploy to confuse rather than clear our understandings. The last thing anybody in Washington wanted the American public to know was that the U.S. government was the father of Terror, that the DoD and CIA funded the terrorists who killed Americans via the Pakistani military. U.S. military and intelligence agencies were the hand; Pakistan's army and military intelligence was the shaft; and radical Islamic jihadi groups were the spearhead. *The war against "Terror" is the war we are waging against ourselves in our transfigured external form. The war on terror is our worst political practices, our wasted taxes, and inhumane methods come back to haunt us.*

I have partially explained the reasons for U.S. involvement in Iraq and Afghanistan but we must look a bit more closely at the logic of capitalism and its contradiction.

Capital: The Tortured, Restless Monstrosity

Great nations are not necessarily "expansionist" by definition. For example, what used to be called the "Great Powers" (Britain, France, Germany, Russia, Italy, and Austria–Hungary) each varied according to expansionist ideals and interests. As Weber pointed out, the

> Their attitude in this respect often changes, and in these changes economic factors play a weighty part … . However, like the Romans, the British, after a short time, were forced out of their policy of self-restraint and pressed into political expansion. This occurred, in part, through capitalist interests in expansion.
>
> (1978: 912)

Not all empires expand for economic reasons but once capitalism has the upper hand it subordinates policy to the interests of development, perpetual growth, accumulation and territorial expansion. "The need of a constantly expanding market for its products chases the bourgeoisie over the whole surface of the globe. It must nestle everywhere, settle everywhere, establish connections everywhere" (Marx and Engels 1977 [1848]: 39). We hear phrases like "economic development" and they seem like they might as well be natural laws that are inherent features of the world around us but we lose sight that these are ideas consciously pursued by particular social classes with specific material interests. Capitalist "development" and "growth" (outward expansion and the reorganization of relations and modes of production) is accompanied by inevitable "violent clashes" (Baran 1957: 4) both internal and external. As a rule, capitalism is incapable of resting on its heels for fear of collapse and its drive forward guarantees a constant pattern of violent conflict. Metaphorically, capitalism is like an undead monster that roams incessantly in search of human life and natural resources to devour.

Capitalism is simply amazing, in every sense of the word—it is truly a thing of wonder and astonishment. No other economic system has managed to create such rapid and wide-reaching social and technological developments as well as staggering oceans of wealth but, all the same, no other economic system that has come before it has been accompanied by such awe-inspiring problems, conflicts, and sheer destructiveness. Baran notes the irony that "the most destructive features of the capitalist order become the very foundations of its continuing existence ..." (1957: xv).

What follows is a summary of just a few serious, interrelated problems associated with capitalism and some ways they relate to our experience of war.

Periodic Economic Crises and Accumulation Problems

We normally associate "economic crises" with events like the Great Depression or "boom and bust cycles," where one minute it seems like everything is going great and then, suddenly, the bottom drops out of the stock market, factories close, and millions of workers are thrown onto the streets. What we fail to realize, with respect to capitalism, is that it goes through accumulation problems from time to time, including a tendency to over-accumulate capital—in a way, the wealthy begin to "drown"in money and they have a problem with keeping it invested in ways that they like (in ways that will make them even wealthier). That was the situation in 2007 when firms found themselves sitting on billions of dollars in cash without good prospects for capital investments in other productive firms or social infrastructure, so they threw that money into wild gambling schemes and complex finance instruments such that rather than investments in "fixed assets" and a better society for all (see Harvey 2003: 181) we find "risk management" schemes that hold on to paper or "liquid" claims to wealth and ownership. This speculative turn began in earnest during the early 1970s and corresponds with both the problem of economic stagnation and challenges to imperial power among periphery nations like those in the Middle East. Our involvement in Iraq is directly related to speculative finance and America's attempt to shore up its global hegemony (see Foster and Magdoff 2009: 75).

Production and Consumption Imbalances

Automated processes have rendered many of our desired goods, consumer electronics for example, virtually free and disposable. So little labor time is required for a robot to make a DVD player that even after manufacturing, transportation, distribution, stocking, and advertising charges are applied, a person can walk out of a store only $20 poorer. The velocity of production means that not only does the amount of labor crystallized in the product fall to virtually nothing (lowering value and prices to rock bottom levels) but it also results in a tendency for the vast over-production of goods. Americans, especially, are awash in consumer goods they cannot buy or use fast enough. Advertising is crucial for stimulating consumption through cultivating feelings of personal dissatisfaction, but production does have a tendency to outstrip consumption. The extension of credit was instrumental throughout the 1980s and 1990s in stimulating the orgy of consumerism but the chickens came home to roost a decade later and Americans are again tightening their belts until better times; when internal consumption and domestic investment become too much of a problem the economic elite turn to external solutions—the annihilation of Iraq serves as one example. Of course, if over-production represents an investment problem then capital funds will be withdrawn from productive firms and injected into paper instruments, leading to a crisis of under-production and rampant speculation. These problems of production lead to a range of other problems such as continuous, violent intrusions around the globe and the cultivation of dependency relations (kick-starting the flow of consumer goods) between core and subaltern nations, e.g., Iraq and the United States.

Structural Unemployment and Underemployment

Unemployment is essential for a normally functioning capitalist labor market. If there are too few workers for available jobs then wages tend to rise (rising wages sounds good to people who work for a living but the more that capitalists spend on wages the less profits end up in their pockets). As of April 2010 the U.S. Bureau of Labor Statistics measured an unemployment rate of 9.9 percent, historically a very high percentage. Of those nearly 10 percent, almost half (45.7 percent) fall into the category of "long-term unemployed," that is, they have been out of work for 27 weeks or more. To be counted on the unemployment rolls, a person has to be actively searching for a job. A person who is unemployed but has given up the hunt does not appear in the numbers. Likewise, a person working even a marginal number of hours does not count as unemployed. Rather, they are underemployed, a condition not much talked about. Of vital interest to young adults entering today's workforce is the condition of being either over-qualified for their positions or working too few hours to earn a descent living. Accompanying "underemployment" is the lack of or limited benefits such as health care, insurance, and job security. Increasingly, workers are being forced to cobble together a string of contingent jobs, each paying low wages and offering little in the way of security. Being a "part-timer" is becoming the norm in the contemporary job market. As of 2009, underemployment impacted about one in six workers. Having abandoned forced conscription in 1973 the U.S. military relies solely on volunteers to populate its ranks. Military pay and food leave much to be desired so compulsion by the "whip of hunger" and unemployment (along with various bribes and incentives) are crucial for enticing America's youth and the unemployable to join. After all, if you have to wear a uniform to work anyway (janitor, fry guy, and so on), a job or career in the military might be preferable.

Over-specialization of Jobs, Deskilling, and Interchangeability

The unity of imaginative and purposeful thought, action, and emotion is what separates humans from other animals. As Marx said,

> what distinguishes the worst architect from the best of bees is that the architect builds the cell in his mind before he constructs it in wax. At the end of every labor process, a result emerges which had already been conceived by the worker at the beginning, hence already existed ideally.
>
> (1976 [1867]: 284)

This special unity (what critical sociologists refer to as "**praxis**") is what we associate with craftsmanship and artisan work and being a creative person in general. "But for men and women," says Braverman,

> any instinctual patterns of work which they may have possessed at the dawn of their evolution have long since atrophied or been submerged by social forms. Thus in humans, as distinguished from animals, the unity between motive force of labor and the labor itself is not inviolable. *The unity of conception and execution may be dissolved.* The conception must still precede and govern execution, but the idea as conceived by *one* may be executed by *another*.
>
> (1974: 50–51)

The trend is toward the development of specialization and then over-specialization of labor to the point where interchangeable, de-skilled, powerless, and low-wage workers twiddle the day away performing mind-numbing tasks that "anybody" could do. This has been an important development for the military where, in the case of unmanned drones, air combat has devolved to video gaming: a "real" pilot performs the "take-off" (and landings) who then passes the flight off to a video gamer who "flies" the craft via satellite, and attack decisions are made by yet another set of individuals. Perhaps in the near future the boundary between fast-food employee and combat pilot will become so blurred that the two jobs become interchangeable.

Class Polarization

From the end of World War II in 1945 to about 1970 the "American Dream" was synonymous with rising wages, job security, leisure and recreation time, home ownership, college education for children, retirement with dignity, etc. Most importantly, we thought of America as the land where the "middle class" was expanding. Since the early 1970s, however, we have witnessed a long-term erosion of the "middle class" such that the incomes and wealth accumulation in the hands of a relatively few families has skyrocketed to unimagined heights while the war on the poor (working and unemployed) along with deindustrialization, outsourced jobs, etc. has meant the implosion of the "middle." The rich get richer and control more of the "economic pie" while the poor get poorer and struggle over an ever-decreasing portion. Interested in continuing their extraction of wealth from the exploitation of the domestic and global work force, the power elite influence, directly and indirectly, the state's policy set to reproduce their rule. Perpetual war and the reproduction of a downwardly mobile and stagnant mass of disposable working-class youth mean the wealthy and the powerful will continue to benefit.

Wage Stagnation and Increasing Household Debt

Overall, the American working class (if you earn a paycheck working for somebody else you are a member of the working class even though you may prefer to think of yourself as "middle class") has not, after accounting for inflation, received a pay raise in more than 40 years. To make up for this stagnation in earnings more household members hit the job market (fewer stay-at-home moms now) and, importantly, families and individuals fell back on easy access to credit to fund their consumption. When their limits were hit and they could not pay back their debt, there was a wave of home refinancing and raiding accumulated equity to fuel more rounds of consumption. When we use credit and loans we are in a sense speculating that our future earnings will be higher than they currently are. For some people and families, their bet pays off, so to speak, but for most, their wages failed to rise as expected. Coupled to variable interest rates on those home-refinancing loans, i.e., the interest rates went way up in the blink of an eye, the lack of expected pay raises made repayments impossible and the housing market collapsed in a tsunami of foreclosures and bankruptcies. If the free market has failed for the bulk of Americans then the lure of an alternative "socialized" system of life awaits those that give up their personal freedoms to serve in the military.

Symbolic Compensations

Are low wages leaving you hungry? Eat some **ideology**. In the face of a steadily declining standard of living Americans are offered symbolic compensations and mechanisms for retaining their sense of identity and entitlements. The proliferation of "title" promotions (jokes abound about all bank employees being "vice presidents" of one thing or another) is only a superficial manifestation of this form of compensation: More troubling is the durability of sexism, racism, homophobia, nationalism, etc. For example, a worker may be underpaid or unemployed or working multiple dead end jobs with no hope of actual socio-economic fulfillment but "at least" he isn't a woman, isn't a foreigner, isn't gay, isn't a communist, and so forth. Note how this logic is reversed (negative) such that the things that matter most are not what one "is" but what one *is not*. This form of thought is synonymous with "**taboo**" consciousness and is the drive behind the allure and fascination that taboo entities and statuses have on conformists, sadists, and destructive personality types. In its "positive" form, symbolic compensations place a value on identifying with some ensemble of representations that signify empowerment and moral rectitude, e.g., American, white, male, straight, conservative, and so on, over all other possible identifications. These "positive" compensations (cynically manipulated by elites and their servants) reinforce nationalist chauvinism, status quo, and reactionary and self-defeating policies. **Patriotism** and gung-ho militarism are also forms of symbolic compensation: it makes some people (the weak and the downtrodden) feel emotionally empowered, strong, and righteous to know that "America" is bombing evil around the world. In short, vile forces such as racism, xenophobia, nationalism, and other forms of symbolic identifications, are synonymous with exploitation (Cassano 2009) and are important forces in cultivating the willing consent of the American public for participating in their own subjugation and are likewise crucial links in solidifying support back home for military adventures around the world (Harvey 2003: 44).

Concentration and Centralization of Wealth and Power

In 2007, the *New York Times* reported:

> Income inequality grew significantly in 2005, with the top 1 percent of Americans —those with incomes that year of more than $348,000—receiving their largest share of national income since 1928, analysis of newly released tax data shows. The top 10 percent, roughly those earning more than $100,000, also reached a level of income share not seen since before the Depression. While total reported income in the United States increased almost 9 percent in 2005, the most recent year for which such data is available, average incomes for those in the bottom 90 percent dipped slightly compared with the year before, dropping $172, or 0.6 percent. The gains went largely to the top 1 percent, whose incomes rose to an average of more than $1.1 million each, an increase of more than $139,000, or about 14 percent. The new data also shows that the top 300,000 Americans collectively enjoyed almost as much income as the bottom 150 million Americans. Per person, the top group received 440 times as much as the average person in the bottom half earned, nearly doubling the gap from 1980.

> (Johnston 2007)

Capital Fetishism and the Politics of Self-defeat

The mystification of capitalism assumes two distinct forms: First, the belief that capitalism is somehow inevitable or natural (like a product of evolution) and, second, that there are somehow two fundamentally different forms of capitalism, one good (productive) and the other risky and morally suspect (finance). Political kooks have harped on this last distinction for decades—most notably during the 1920s and 1930s when reactionary theologians, Nazis, fascist, etc., bashed finance as Jewish and therefore un-Christian (Worrell 1999). This propensity to perceive finance as a separate species of capital was addressed by Marx in his discussion of interest-bearing capital. Marx's term for this compartmentalization was "capital **fetishism**" (Marx 1981 [1894]: 515–24, 968; see also Massing 1949: 13).

In volume three of *Capital*, Marx indicates, "In interest-bearing capital, the capital relationship reaches its most superficial and fetishized form. Here we have *M–M'*, money that produces more money, self-valorizing value, without the process that mediates the two extremes" (1981 [1894]: 515). If the ruling elite, mainstream politicians, and the business media can convince the voters of Western democracies there exists no difference between finance and speculation, that finance can be rehabilitated, and that capitalism is normal and good, indeed, red-blooded Americanism, then people will feel good about defending "free markets," "free enterprise," etc., on the world's battlefields. Illustrating perfectly what we mean by "capital fetishism" Leicht and Fitzgerald indicate that, election after election, as the American working and "middle" classes sink further into the abyss, absolutely no discussion of capitalism is permitted by either mainstream political party; the role of identity or "displacement" politics is crucial in solidifying the domination of capital over the public:

> the politics of displacement is routinely played out in our legislative bodies any time proposals for tangible improvements to middle-class life reach the limelight. Want to talk about healthcare for all? Sidetrack the discussion by bringing up abortion and stem cell research that "they" want. Want to talk about family-friendly social policies like family leave and childcare subsidies? Rant instead about gay marriage … . Want to discuss why American corporations export jobs overseas and hire illegal immigrants here at home? Sidetrack the discussion by mentioning how much unemployment an increase in the minimum wage would bring.
>
> (Leicht and Fitzgerald 2007: 146)

Dependency and the Instrumentalization of Human Life

Arguably, the most disturbing aspect of capitalism is the reduction of human life to the status of tools or instruments. Most people would tell you that they consider human life more important than material goods or cash but, in practice, capitalist economies reverse these ideals: Having a job means that you are used as an instrument (a means) to another end (money). In a sense, having a job (working for somebody else because you do not own your own means of subsistence) means that you live so that another may enjoy at your expense. How? We just have to separate out the notions of your private existence and your public function.

As a private person with your own life you have aspirations, dreams, goals and individual desires that you want to satisfy. Your life is an end in itself. But your public role or function, being an employee for example, means that you normally have to set aside individual interests (except the need for money) for the sake of what your employer wants of you—your boss does not want the "whole you," just your time, energy, and the particular skills that pertain to your job. For most of us, then, the job inverts our existence to the role of an animate tool. Wage stagnation and credit peonage ensure that we will have to dedicate more of our time and energy in serving an employer—you remain an individual human being in your own "free" time but your social time, your time on the job, the time you spend performing your social role, converts the human being into something more akin to an animal that pulls a cart for its master. And, of course, this "instrumentalization" of life applies to the "others" that inhabit our world.

With the fusion of capital and foreign policy comes the division of the world into those that are "with us" and those that are "against us"—those that are on "our side" will be used as tools to further the U.S. agenda and those that are "other" will be subjected to force. Since the end of the Cold War political-economic survival has depended upon a nation's ability to be useful and profitable for the U.S.—buying U.S. debt, paying extortion money, unimpeded flow of commodities, and crushing internal insurgencies that challenge the rule of the U.S.

Here we begin to transition from the "economic" to the "political" aspects of war. The currents of natural energy and political power are woven together by massive corporations and the drive for capital accumulation. During the Cold War the various "third world" countries could play the U.S. and the USSR against one another, seeking the best deals. Since 1991, however, the U.S. has played hardball, imposing its will on the rest of the world. As we will see, though, the United States has set a course that may well fail. Over-extended financially and militarily in the Middle East after September 11 the U.S. now faces serious challenges to its continued hegemony—indeed, the reign of America over the rest of the world may be coming to an end.

Tribute, Coercion, and Dollarization

C. Wright Mills argued a long time ago that business and governance were so interconnected that "The two cannot now be seen clearly as two distinct worlds" (1956: 274). When it comes to war, today, economics and politics are *identical*. As we saw with Iraq, capitalist **imperialism** of the American style "amounts to foisting insti-tutional arrangements and conditions upon others, usually in the name of universal well-being … . The United States will deliver this gift of freedom (of the market) to the world whether it likes it or not" (Harvey 2003: 133). But it appears that the global imperial system, with the United States as the core actor, is not going unchallenged. Indeed, we may be witnessing the shifting of power from the West to the East: from the U.S. "towards Asia as the hegemonic center of global power. It is unlikely that the US will go quietly and peacefully into that goodnight" (Harvey 2003: 77). The American military machine is now kept in a permanent state of "police actions" around the planet "looking to flex military muscle as the only clear absolute power it has left … [hiding] the exaction of tribute from the rest of the world under a rhetoric of deliver-ing peace and freedom for all" (Harvey 2003: 77).

Remember, the United States used to be a major industrial manufacturer and exporter of manufactured goods. Our cities used to center around factories, mills, and mines. For the most part, those days are gone. What does the U.S. export except a hail of gunfire? Today, America's greatest export is the $100 bill.

> The **Bretton Woods** agreement of 1944 [which created the International Mon-etary Fund (IMF) and the World Bank] turned the dollar into the world's reserve currency and tied the world's economic development firmly into US fiscal and monetary policy. The United States acted as the world's banker in return for an opening up of the world's commodity and capital markets to the power of the large corporations.
>
> (Harvey 1990: 137)

One of Iraq's infractions was a publicized plan to denominate its oil reserves in euros instead of dollars. This threat to U.S. power had to be put down as a lesson to other nations contemplating a switch from the dollar to other currencies:

> dollar hegemony is precisely what the invasion of Iraq is all about. Indeed, the most striking feature of the current world economic conjuncture is the large and growing imbalances on external account between the major economies. The World Economic Outlook of the International Monetary Fund (IMF) issued in January 2003, had a detailed, if finally rather superficial, analysis of this question. It iden-tified the main deficit countries as Australia, New Zealand, Britain and the U.S. These four … countries, in other words, constitute one pole of the growing imbal-ances in the global economy. Take away New Zealand from this group and the 'coalition of the willing' that invaded Iraq begins to acquire quite another identity: the 'coalition of the terminally bankrupt.'
>
> (Muralidharan 2003)

A key function of U.S. military prowess is to discipline nations with regard to their monetary and financial policies. Nothing says "obey, or else" like a naval battle group conducting "exercises" just off your shores. Dealing in dollars, the use of the dollar as the global medium of exchange (making it the currency of account) ensures that the federal government can continue deficit spending while keeping taxes low for the wealthy and powerful corporations. In a clear sign, however, that the U.S. may well be on the cusp of a complete financial implosion is the persistence of rival power blocs to defy the dollar. China, Russia, Japan, France, Brazil, and a coalition of Arab gulf states are currently engaged in joint discussions centered around ending their dependence on U.S. dollars and conducting energy transactions using a "basket of currencies" consisting of the euro, the Japanese yen, the Chinese yuan, gold, and a proposed unified Gulf state common currency (Fisk 2009). This "war" of currencies provides a partial but important backdrop for the development of two distinct forms of state-capital relationships: the capitalized state (U.S.) going up against new state capitalist regimes in China, Russia and elsewhere.

DISCUSSION QUESTIONS

1. What is the relationship between war and the accumulation of wealth?
2. Is war a business like any other business?
3. How is war situated in relationship to other socio-economic problems like unemployment and under-consumption?
4. What is the connection between the way fast-food jobs are designed and the way modern wars are conducted?

IV: Geopolitical and Ideological Aspects of War

⮞⬥⮜

The United States made its bid for global dominance in the aftermath of World War II when it initiated a nuclear showdown with the Soviet Union. Since the collapse of the USSR and the "winning" of the Cold War by the U.S., the role of the state and its relationship to capital has been radically transformed. A host of "state capitalist" regimes (China, Russia, etc.) pose challenges to America's system of global domination. No longer a mediator between the interests of capital and the needs of labor, the state has been reduced to a police force and ministry of "propaganda" for use on other nations as well as against its own citizens.

The Atomic Bomb and World War II

Modern military strategy revolves around fancy weapons, the existence of which should be enough to deter enemy attack, or, in the event of hostilities, can be used at a distance, reducing the exposure of American forces to hostile fire and reducing the number of troops necessary to carry the fight to the enemy. The ultimate expression of that philosophy is the nuclear weapon, the first of which were the two atomic bombs that the U.S. dropped on Japan at the end of World War II. During the Cold War, nuclear weapons were deployed around the globe, undergirding a philosophy of deterrence. In 1960 nuclear weapons were the building blocks of a master plan for dealing with Soviet aggression. The Single Integrated Operational Plan (SIOP) basically meant launching the "entire strategic force of about 3,500 nuclear weapons against the Soviet Union, China and satellite states" (Hoffman 2009: 15–16). The administration was concerned with "overkill" but in reality detonating that many warheads would have triggered a **nuclear winter** and led to the almost immediate extinction of all human life on the planet. SIOP was revised, serving as the precursor of another plan of "assured destruction" (also known as MAD, or mutually assured destruction) whereby the U.S. and the Soviets would aim so many weapons at each other that any preemptive strike would spell certain doom for all humanity thus "assuring" that no attacks would be forthcoming (Hoffman 2009: 16–17).

One legacy of the Cold War is that today several nations besides the U.S. and Russia own nuclear weapons: France, England, China, India, Pakistan, Israel, and North

Korea with other nations allowing nuclear weapons to be based on their soil. That China, Pakistan, and India possess nukes is one reason the U.S. has set up bases in Iraq and will maintain a permanent, active presence in the region. Americans have been taught that the nuclear bomb is some kind of "last resort" that would only be used as a last ditch effort to defend the nation. That line of reasoning does not quite fit the facts however. Not only did America unnecessarily deploy two bombs on Japan in 1945, the Eisenhower administration offered France two nuclear bombs to use against communist forces at Dien Bien Phu (Vietnam) in 1954 and, in 1969, the Nixon administration contemplated using nuclear weapons to end U.S. involvement in Vietnam. We can learn much about the American attitude toward "the bomb" and its role in foreign relations by examining in some detail the reasoning behind the decision to subject the Japanese to these weapons.

Americans were told that the use of atomic weapons against Japan at the end of World War II was regrettable but necessary because our determined enemy would fight to the last man and that, even though the bombs killed a staggering number of people (approximately 200,000), even more, on both sides, would have died if our troops had been required to fight all the way to Tokyo. A new generation of scholars has challenged our received wisdom. In the words of General Eisenhower, Supreme Allied Commander, the Japanese "were already defeated and … dropping the bomb was completely unnecessary" (in Jarecki 2008: 63). Japanese diplomatic and operational codes had been broken by cryptanalysts (Sayle 1995) and "declassified Japanese telegraphs intercepted at that time showed that [President] Truman and his advisers surely knew by 1945 that the Japanese were earnestly seeking a mediated end to the war" (Jarecki 2008: 63). General Grove, the commander of America's new atomic forces (roughly two dozen bombers and two bombs) actually feared that the Japanese would surrender *before* the bombs could be used and thereby sped up development and testing accordingly (Sayle 1995: 54). Additionally, neither of the cities bombed were legitimate military targets—at least 90 percent of the dead were civilians—and their destruction did not contribute to a degradation of Japan's combat capabilities. If the decision to use atomic weapons against the Japanese over the cities of Hiroshima and Nagasaki were militarily indefensible what purpose did they serve?

The purpose the bombs served was demonstrating to the Soviet Union who was going to be the unrivaled global power in the post-war era (Alperovitz 1996). "The real motive," says Smith,

> was to prevent Soviet influence on settlement of the Pacific War. The ending of the war by such means and solely on U.S. terms advertised the fact that instruments of genocide had become a prerequisite to effective power, setting off a world-wide arms race that plagues humanity to this day, with no end in sight. The painstaking progress that nations had made in preventing war from descending into random

extermination was thus rather casually discarded, an abandonment that portended doom for innumerable innocents in Asia, Africa, and Latin America.

(Smith 2001: 17)

Japan was an object lesson in what would happen to the Soviets and their allies if U.S. supremacy in the post-war era were to be challenged.

The bombings of Hiroshima and Nagasaki were not the final days of World War II, but instead the opening shots in the Cold War (Jarecki 2008). The Soviet Union has since been dismantled but we are still dealing with the reverberations of the collapse of that empire. The countries of central Asia, formerly contained within the Soviet system, are now desperate to get their energy reserves (oil and gas) onto the international markets via proposed pipelines that would have to run through a highly unstable and unpredictable Afghanistan. As we have seen, energy and oil were important considerations that factored into the U.S. decision to level Iraq. But there were other, perhaps equally important factors, like dollarization, that we have touched on. The dollarization program (organizing global finances at the end of World War II around the U.S. dollar and thereby solidifying U.S. leadership over international trade) marked a crucial mechanism that would help to sustain continued U.S. global dominance even after it had relinquished its role as major industrial power.

Capital–State Convergence

In some countries capitalists own their own state, using it as an instrument of class domination, and in other countries the state keeps a tight reign on business and capital ownership. In the U.S. we have seen the penetration of the state by capitalist firms and financial interests to such a point that the federal and state governments, to a great extent, function as the handmaids of corporations and Wall Street. Check out who the major contributors are to presidential elections. When something is "too big to fail" rest assured it is not the mass of everyday Americans but some investment firm. For more than 30 years the state has energetically squeezed its own citizens, the working and 'middle' classes, for the purpose of enriching a minority of society's members—so few, in fact, that in a society of more than 300 million members, their wealthy rulers could easily fit into a single concert hall. In China, Russia, and some Arab monarchies, by contrast, the dynamic power of capitalism is harnessed by authoritarian political regimes in an effort to increase and solidify their control—what Bremmer (2010) and others refer to as "state capitalism."

We saw earlier in this book that in the U.S., beginning in the late 1970s and rolling along unabated for 40 years, the wealthiest Americans and large corporations were relieved of their public obligations and the burdens of sharing. The massive transfer of wealth from ordinary Americans into the pockets of the corporate elite was facilitated by a reorganized state that was no longer constituted by the people, for the people. Political actors used their offices to enrich their corporate masters and themselves as corporate executives (e.g., former Vice President Dick Cheney), resulting in what Bremmer calls a state of "**hypercapitalism**."

> The term *hypercapitalism* refers to a situation in which an unregulated market overheats in a wave of unchecked but irrational exuberance. In these cases, it is mistakenly believed that money, rather than wealth, creates more wealth; that financial practices should be given free rein to create monetary value with as little government involvement as possible; and that additional monetary value does not need to be backed by proportionate increases in real economic productivity.
>
> (Bremmer 2010: 47)

Hypercapitalism certainly suffered a public relations setback in recent years but we should expect more of the same for the foreseeable future. For decades the power elite in the U.S. viewed the state as a problem not a solution and, for the most part, that view has not changed. What was important, among all state functions, was a sharp stick—the military and intelligence elements that would, first, defeat communism and then assist transnational capital in conquering and subduing the planet. In places like China, Russia, and elsewhere, a quite different attitude toward the state prevailed and these regimes are now using their state powers to challenge American global dominance.

In the general sense, "state capitalism" represents the "next step" in the development of capitalism from private ownership of the means of production to a new type of ownership. The profit motive is still vital and central and, importantly, this new form is not identical with socialism (Pollock 1982 [1941]: 72). In its totalitarian form,

> "the state is the power instrument of a new ruling group, which has resulted from the merger of the most powerful vested interests, the top-ranking personnel in industrial and business management, the higher strata of the state bureaucracy (including the military) and the leading figures of the victorious party's bureaucracy." In the democratic form of state capitalism "the state has the same controlling functions [as it does in the totalitarian form] but is itself controlled by the people."
>
> (Pollock 1982 [1941]: p. 73)

What conservative defenders of capitalism like Ian Bremmer (quoted above) fail to realize is that the U.S. is now itself predominantly a *mixture* of "spectacular" finance adventurism (what Bremmer calls "hypercapitalism") and a blending of the democratic *and* totalitarian forms of state capitalism. What makes American state capitalism democratic is that the public still elects its political leadership. What makes it partially totalitarian is that virtually all of the elected political leaders are fully under the command of capital, bought and paid for by corporations, working in allegiance with finance, speculators, and transnational firms. Given the current composition of the state the future of international warfare will look a lot like it does now in Afghanistan: An endless string of battles and firefights between troops from core state coalitions against terrorists and jihadists backed up by rogue authoritarian regimes.

China, Russia, and other big state actors have watched the U.S. sinking into what may turn out to be another military quagmire (Afghanistan) that it is no closer to 'winning' than it was when it started. These states have also grown weary of U.S. financial domination and the dangers associated with irresponsible speculation enabled by Washington. We now see states pulling back from commitments to free market principles, taking back control of their resources (disobedience that would previously have resulted in a prompt beat down by the State Department, CIA, and DoD), and setting in place new international barriers and 'rigidities' that will create more accumulation problems for Wall Street and Washington. As the U.S. state is stymied in its external relations it will have to ramp up oppression at home in order to extract more internal wealth and check possible disorder.

State Security and Secrecy

As we saw earlier, post-Fordism represents a regime of capital accumulation that hinges on the notion of "flexibility"—i.e., the loss of full-time, permanent jobs characterized by high wages, benefits, vertical career ladders, etc., and their replacement by part-time jobs that combine low wages and few benefits with insecurity. On college and university campuses you can see this all around you: The evaporation of tenured and tenure-track faculty and their replacement with adjuncts and other part-timers working for peanuts. Other aspects of "post-Fordism" are the diminishment of manufacturing, outsourcing jobs overseas, a war on organized labor, high rates of inmate incarceration, the growth of domestic security mechanisms and a highly punitive criminal justice system, stagnant wages, high rates of underemployment, privatization of the public assets, the ascendency of speculation (financial gambling) over solid capital investments, the high value of spectacle and entertainment, and so on. As Harvey says, this climate of insecurity and the importance of aesthetics and surface images and rhetoric coincide with "a climate conducive to authoritarianism of the Thatcher–Reagan type …" or what others have called "'the friendly face of fascism'" (1990: 168, 330). It wasn't for nothing that Prime Minister Margaret Thatcher's nickname was "The Iron Lady" and "Attila the Hen."

During the Cold War it was the threat of communism that drove American obsessions with loyalty and secrecy "and the consequent need to keep our 'secrets' … has been used as justification for exacting conformity from the American people" (Lens

1987: 44). In the absence of the command to conform we hear, today, that Americans and their allies need to establish a "consensus" regarding the use of force and suppression. With communism down and out, it is "Terror" and "Evil" (vastly more abstract and therefore capable of inducing even more fear) that justifies secrecy and a conformity reflex amongst the populace. The continuous build-up of what Lens refers to as the "National Security State" leads inexorably to the development of a vast authoritarian info-political mechanism that is terrifying in size and complexity, including familiar entities like the Department of Homeland Security, FBI, CIA, National Security Administration (NSA), Defense Intelligence Agency (DIA) as well as a web of nebulous and rumored organizations. This ever-proliferating body of intelligence and security organizations combined with the intensified drive toward secrecy means that regulation and transparent oversight become impossible or, at best, extremely difficult. Simply put: We cannot apply the rule of law or rationally govern that which we know nothing about, or are intentionally kept in the dark about. All we would have to go on is blind trust and Americans learned long ago that the federal government is far from trustworthy. If the state manages to act in a highly undemocratic fashion it begs the question of the nature of social psychology and political legitimacy in contemporary American society. The state can only act badly if we allow it to, so why do we allow it to? On the one hand, we can approach this as a problem of ideology.

> The concept of "ideology" reflects the one discovery which emerged from political conflict, namely, that ruling groups can in their thinking become so intensively interest-bound to a situation that they are simply no longer able to see certain facts which would undermine their sense of domination.

> (Mannheim 1936: 40)

The actions of Bush and his neo-con advisers offer a good example of such ideological action. Not only were they "blind" to facts that undermined their case for war in Iraq but they also concocted "facts" to fit their agenda. And this "particularistic" aspect of ideology (conscious manipulations and calculations) fits with the overall or "total" ideological environment within which the U.S. operates: That the U.S. is morally good in all that it does, that it is morally justified in using force in whatever it sets out to do, that free markets are best for everyone, that the U.S. knows what is best for other peoples, etc., in short, that there is one good social order (ours) that is right for every person on earth. Ideologies are not simply dropped on us; we ourselves are ideological creations. If the state security apparatus represents a colossal authoritarian threat then it must legitimate itself by either lying about its intentions or, conversely, legitimate itself on the basis of what it is: Authoritarian. I think it does both.

For an authoritarian society to flourish it needs not only to claim to be engaged in a great and good humanitarian project that will benefit all of mankind (read the

White House's 2010 "National Security Strategy" for a full dose) but a great many of its members must also embody, more or less, the spirit of authoritarianism and an excitement for conflict. How does the state communicate all this to the public? Assuming the public is interested it gets its political information primarily from corporate media.

Corporate Media and "Embedded" Journalism

1896 represents one of those rare moments when "everything" seems to change. Not only was this the year of the "first mass circulation daily newspaper, *The Daily Mail*" (England) but also the cinematograph, and "wireless telegraphy." "In one remarkable year," says Taylor,

> the principal means of mass communication—press, radio, and film—came into their own and the communications revolution made a quantum leap. It was the convergence of total war and the mass media that gave modern war propaganda its significance and impact in the twentieth century.
>
> (Taylor 1990: 162)

We might naturally assume that journalism, news, and the media in general have no vested interest in war and, instead, just report whatever is going on in the world. However, the manufacturers of news (news is a commodity after all) have known for decades that war amounts to an instant boost in sales and revenue streams.

> The Press lives by advertising; advertising follows circulation, and circulation depends on excitement. "What sells a newspaper?" … The first answer is "war." War not only creates a supply of news but a demand for it. So deep-rooted is the fascination in war and all things appertaining to it that … a paper has only to be able to put up on its placard "A Great Battle" for its sales to mount up. This is the key to the proclivity of the Press to aggravate public anxiety in moments of crises.
>
> (Lasswell 1971: 192)

Far from giving us the straight scoop, according to Lasswell, the press actually sets out to induce anxiety within the minds of readers and viewers. As such, the press contributes to rather than moderates the effects of propaganda. Jacques Ellul points to this paradox: The more viewpoints and news sources we have available to us, the more we are divided from one another, hermetically sealed off as it were, from divergent opinions and perspectives until, finally, we "cease altogether to be open to an exchange of reason, arguments, points of view" (1965: 213). If the partitioning of perspectives was a problem before, the Internet has created not only new opportunities for mental exploration but actually created an exponentially worse form of mental tribalism.

The era of digital information has not only contributed to an enhanced "tribalism" but also the near-extinction of investigative journalism. As newspapers shrink and staff are reduced to skeleton crews the very expensive and time-consuming work of investigations into political corruptions and lies is cut and replaced by fluff pieces and opinion editorials. Lacking the ability to generate its own content, corporate media relies increasingly on press releases by the state. "Control of information gives the American government the ability to manufacture public opinion" (Lens 1987: 122) and the "official line" (could be outright lies and propaganda for all we know) becomes "news" and "factual." Even when the media is doing its best to present factual news it is already hobbled by the limitations of journalism.

> Because journalists are neither sociologists nor historians, their concern is more with the detail than the overall picture. They work for news organizations the role of which is to bring to the public the extraordinary rather than the typical … perhaps the biggest casualty of all in wartime news reporting, focusing as it does on the spectacular incident or speech around which the story can be framed, is context.
>
> (Taylor 1998: 13)

Since the first Gulf War (1990–91) the DoD has organized and controlled the media "pools" that accompany troops into combat, framing what the reporters see, spinning interpretations, and then sanitizing the reports they file so as to not compromise operational security. Even if reporters could transmit reliable information to their editors, there is little chance that anything truly critical can make its way to the general public. When we examine the composition of the "interlocking directorate" (the network of power and leadership relations) it is troubling to find movers and shakers in the world of finance, defense and aerospace, and media moguls sitting next to one another in boardrooms making decisions that will send young men and women off to die.

DISCUSSION QUESTIONS

1. Why did the U.S. drop atomic bombs on Japan at the end of World War II?
2. Is America a "'state capitalist" nation and, if so, what kind?
3. How are concerns over "security" and the need for "secrecy" undermining democracy?
4. Can big corporate and government-controlled news sources deliver the kind of information to the American public needed to make informed decisions?

V: The Social and Cultural Elements of War

~~~~~~~~~~~

War is not a natural fact of human life; it is a social phenomenon. We are not doomed outright to perpetual war but are socialized to accept and glorify war and hate others who are not like us. Propaganda, patriotism, nationalism, and war are used as instruments of social control in times of crisis and, most importantly, to legitimate undemocratic methods and objectives pursued by the state.

Are Humans Hardwired for Violence and Aggression?

Rousseau correctly observed that people "are not naturally enemies" but that "conflicts over things" and the struggle over property and resources are what drive people to war (1968 [1762]: 55). Since Rousseau's time, social scientists have put to rest the erroneous biological assumptions regarding anything like a natural or built-in inclination toward war. Humans are definitely not hardwired for something like war and there is nothing genetic about war.

War is definitely not inevitable. War is highly variable across time and place. While war is a very old phenomenon, its practice in ancient and "primitive" societies was very different from what we think of as war today. We used to imagine that "primitives" were bloodthirsty savages and that civilization and technological innovations and progress have moderated our natural inclinations to kill. However, exactly the opposite is true: Wars are more frequent and more destructive with the development of civilization and technological progress (Fromm 1973). If we have an interest in circumventing war and conflict in the future we must carefully think about how we educate and socialize our children. Soldiers are not born but made, and without willing and enthusiastic participants on the part of the general populace, wars will be impossible to wage.

Socialization for War: Sadism, Destructiveness, and Conformity

Living and working in postmodern America, with its high unemployment, dead-end jobs, diminishing life chances, and mindless entertainment and credit consumption makes some of us feel small, weak, and worthless.

The enduring attraction of war is this: Even with its destruction and carnage it can give us what we long for in life. It can give us purpose, meaning, a reason for living. Only when we are in the midst of conflict does the shallowness … of our lives become apparent. Trivia dominates our conversations and increasingly our airwaves. And war is an enticing elixir. It gives us resolve, a cause. It allows us to be noble. And those who have the least meaning in their lives, the impoverished refugees in Gaza, the disenfranchised North African immigrants in France, even the legions of young who live in the splendid indolence and safety of the industrialized world, are all susceptible to war's appeal.

(Hedges 2002: 3–4)

No longer content with mere "trivia," today's citizen prefers scandal and outrage, spectacle and the biggest lies.

David Harvey notes that today, in our "postmodern" world, we consciously love ideology and political spectacle that we go so far as to revel in "the activity of masking and cover-up, all the fetishisms of locality, place, or social grouping, while denying that kind of meta-theory which can grasp the political-economic processes … that are becoming ever more universalizing in their depth, intensity, reach and power over daily life" (1990: 117). Are people merely stupid and enjoy their degradation or is there some explanation for why people would willingly consent to their manipulation? In a way, if we are lied to we can rationalize our own self-destructive participation. I can tell myself I am going to Iraq to help "rebuild" and do something "for my country" when in fact I am only going for the higher wages that I can no longer find at home. I can join the Army and "give something back to my country" and rationalize away the fact that my country provided so little by way of opportunity that it was either the Army or the unemployment line. When we suffer setbacks, as individuals or as a nation, we can fall back on a myth that has kept us going since our colonial days: *the destruction of the other can save us.*

The first colonists saw in America an opportunity to regenerate their fortunes, their spirits, and the power of their church and nation; but the means to that regeneration ultimately became the means of violence, and the myth of regeneration through violence became the structuring metaphor of the American experience."

(Slotkin 1973: 5)

Life in an economically reckless society can lead individuals to feel powerless, isolated, and searching for a meaning to existence. Since self-fulfillment in work is generally blocked and skills for self-expression have melted away through over-specialized tasks and pre-made cultural consumption, the autonomous and fully developed *self* (the crowning achievement of modern society) is under-developed. The alternate routes open to the thwarted life and high levels of anxiety involve the renunciation of personal freedom "and to try to overcome ... aloneness by eliminating the gap that has arisen between ... [the] individual self and the world" (Fromm 1941: 139). Fromm identified three social-psychological dynamics or "mechanisms of escape" that go a long way in explaining self-destructive conduct and the attempts to discharge anxiety: authoritarianism, destructiveness, and automaton conformity.

Psychological authoritarianism (another term for social sadomasochism) is the desire to submit to something or obey somebody recognized as a higher authority or legitimate power—e.g., the president, populist leader, god, or something abstract like "the American way." Authoritarians also combine submissiveness with a drive to subordinate and control groups or individuals who are weaker and imagined to be morally inferior. An orientation toward strength and weakness, submission and domination, are the essential aspects of the authoritarian personality. Some researchers add a dimension of "conventionality" to these two essential traits such that the authoritarian exhibits "a high degree of adherence to the social conventions that are perceived to be endorsed by society and its established authorities" (Altemeyer 1996: 6). The authoritarian personality is basically a fascist ready to be activated by the right command and under the right circumstances. Are there a lot of potential fascists in the U.S.? Every credible study over the last 60 years points to the existence of deep and wide currents of authoritarianism in our society.

Destructiveness seeks not to bond with something higher and stronger while controlling or dominating something lower and weaker but tries to escape from the anguish and anxiety of the external world by destroying it or engaging in self-destructive actions in the absence of external threats (Fromm 1941: 177–83). In the U.S., our team sports and popular culture suffer from a high level of "necrophilia" or love of decay, killing, destroying, and eliminating problems through force.

Automaton conformity is the solution adopted by "normal" people: He or she

> adopts entirely the kind of personality offered to him by cultural patterns; and he therefore becomes exactly as all others are and as they expect him to be. The discrepancy between "I" and the world disappears and with it the conscious fear of aloneness and powerlessness ... . The person who gives up his individual self and becomes an automaton, identical with millions of other automatons around him, need not feel alone and anxious any more. But the price he pays, however, is high; it is the loss of his self.

> (Fromm 1941: 184)

The pure automaton is difficult to find in reality; even in the military there were few (but some) who approach the model of the human robot. But what is undeniably true is, while human robots are uncommon, conformism is real and stifles self-development, creativity, and our chances for personal freedom. People and groups that suffer from some blending of authoritarianism, destructiveness, and conformity make easy prey of political propaganda that divides the world up into the strong and the weak, objects of hatred deserving of annihilation, and demanding obedience and conformity as a precondition for being accepted.

Us vs. Them, Good vs. Evil, Friend vs. Enemy

"War makes the world understandable, a black and white tableau of them and us. It suspends thought, especially self-critical thought. All bow before the supreme effort" (Hedges 2002: 10). President George W. Bush startled the world in his September 20, 2001 address to a joint session of Congress and the American people when he proclaimed "Every nation, in every region, now has a decision to make. Either you are with us, or you are with the terrorists." In other words, you will support the decisions of the White House and the conduct of the U.S. military or you are a candidate for destruction. Not only does this kind of divisive rhetoric put a damper on criticism and rational thought and discourse but it also harkens back to an older style of dividing the world up into binary poles of good versus evil, us versus them. This line of persuasion placed Bush in the odious company of a long line of political strategists, most notably, perhaps, the influential Carl Schmitt, a political philosopher for the Nazis; influential not only for his role in the formation of Nazi political ideology but a fairly clear line of descent can be drawn linking Schmitt to the now-discredited neoconservative architects of America's adventure in Iraq.

The essence of Schmitt's concept of politics can be summarized for our purposes in his own words:

> The specific political distinction to which political actions and motives can be reduced is that between friend and enemy … . The political enemy need not be morally evil or aesthetically ugly; he need not appear as an economic competitor, and it may even be advantageous to engage with him in business transactions. But he is, nevertheless, the other, the stranger; and it is sufficient for his nature that he is, in a specially intense way, existentially something different and alien, so that in the extreme case conflicts with him are possible.
>
> (Schmitt 1996 [1932]: 26–27)

In other words, sociologically, people are not enemies based upon the fact that they *are* "existentially something different and alien"—rather, people *become* something other, that is "different and alien" (and accordingly a targetable enemy to be defeated in armed conflict) because they are constructed as such within a ritualized and rhetorical system of propaganda and symbolic manipulation. Schmitt's definition of the political as the delineation between friend and enemy is perfectly attuned to the logic of propaganda and may even reduce politics to propaganda pure and simple. Here, we can draw a line from enemy construction to the reduction of politics to propaganda via the idea of ideology. As Mannheim says, "it is only when the distrust of man toward man, which is more or less evident at every stage of human history, becomes explicit and is methodically recognized, that we may properly speak of an ideological taint in the utterances of others" (1936: 61); from distrust, to enemies, to ideologies, to propaganda.

"In all propaganda," says Keen, "the face of the enemy is designed to provide a focus for our hatred. He is the other. The outsider. The alien. He is not human" (1986: 16). Schmitt did not insist that the "enemy" was also necessarily an object of hatred but he was also not a sociologist or anthropologist. As soon as groups divide the world up between the "inside" and the "outside"—the "Us" and the "Them," etc.—the stage is set for the demonization of the alien representation. "All propaganda" says Ellul "has to set off its group from all the other groups. Here we find again the fallacious character of the intellectual communication media (press, radio), which, far from uniting people and bringing them closer together, divide them all the more" (1965: 212). It is important that we remember that enemies are not what they seem to be on the surface. Emile Durkheim, the founder of modern sociology, hit the nail on the head when he wrote that today's relation is tomorrow's "dreaded enemy." We do not demonize a group through political propaganda because they are enemies; the other becomes an enemy because they are targets of our propaganda. We undeniably have enemies but *we make them ourselves* (1995: 404–05). There can be no demons without the act of demonization. Demonization and political propaganda means that we turn others into one-dimensional caricatures, we reduce humans to non-human things, meaning that we can easily overlook our material and political relationship to the other (how is our way of life transforming or hurting their way of life?) and then use deadly force against them. And, of course, in times of trouble, when all the elements of propaganda are in full bloom, the "patriotic" citizen is expected to obey his or her leaders. "In all hierarchically structured societies obedience is perhaps the most deeply ingrained trait. Obedience is equated with virtue, disobedience with sin" (Fromm 1973: 207).

Unfortunately, being a "patriot" has become synonymous with blind obedience.

> Patriotism, often a thinly veiled form of collective self-worship, celebrates our goodness, our ideals, our mercy, and bemoans the perfidiousness of those who hate us. Never mind the murder and repression done in our name by bloody sur-rogates from the Shah of Iran to the Congolese dictator ... Mobotu, who received from Washington well over a billion dollars in civilian and military aid during the three decades of his rule"
>
> (Hedges 2002: 10).

Wanting to appear "patriotic," we heed the call to sacrifice and tolerate indiscriminant violence. If a person truly loved his or her country they would demand transparency and accountability on the part of their elected officials and would not succumb to cheap tricks on the part of cynical politicians who use their positions within the state to increase their wealth and power and who use flowery rhetoric about peace and democracy to legitimate malevolent intentions.

Max Weber found that during World War I all political "parties sharing in the government become 'patriotic'" (1978: 1426). We saw this after 9/11 when few politicians from either side of the aisle dared to resist the lure of military retaliation for fear of appearing weak and because of the potential for voter backlash. Fear of weakness, blind patriotism, and nationalism all conspire to render the American public an easy victim for exploitation.

Nationalism entails several generic features common to all particular nationalist forms. According to Gelvin (2008: 197–98) these features include:

- The belief that "humanity" is less than or equal to the sum of its parts, i.e., "humanity is naturally divided into smaller units, or nations."
- The idea that all nations have unique and essential characteristics such as language, traditions, religious beliefs, and so on "that all its citizens hold in common."
- The notion that surface appearances change over time but the essential core features of a nation remain unchanged.
- The assumption that a nation is inherently linked to a particular geographical place or land.
- The belief that nations have unique and common interests and the state's role is to promote those interests.

"In the modern world," says Gelvin, "these assumptions need no explanation or justification. They just *are*. And the very fact that they appear obvious and commonsensical means that nationalism, when used in its most general sense, might be called an 'ideology'" (2008: 198). Most disturbing, perhaps, is not that the "ideology of nationalism transforms subjects into citizens" but that it transforms "citizens into cogs of a machine grinding away for something called 'the common good' (or common wealth)" (Gelvin 2008: 199).

Extraordinary Situations, Excitement, and the Sleep of Reason

Going to war, being attacked by an external enemy, disasters of one kind or another, etc., can be classified as "extraordinary situations" that produce widespread excitement or enthusiasm and also high levels of anxiety among a population. In these decisive moments the normal forms of law, customs, and values can be "inverted" or "overthrown" (Weber 1978: 1117) whereby a population simply suspends, at least temporarily, its usual standards of reasonable reflection, inquiry, accountability, and rational procedures and instituted processes. In other words, the extraordinary or exceptional historical moment may unleash a flood of charisma, hysteria, and irrationality. When a group, cohort, nation, etc., is enthralled by the promises and perceived strength of a charismatic leader, they "surrender ... to the extraordinary and unheard-of, to what is alien to all regulation and tradition and therefore is viewed as divine—surrender which arises from distress or enthusiasm" (Weber 1978: 1115). This "enthusiasm" or collective excitement is what the sociologist Emile Durkheim called "collective effervescence."

A society caught up in the heat of the moment is liable to throw caution to the wind, get carried away, and do things that are counterproductive and self-destructive. To the extent that we are "excited" and make our moves based on fear and limited understanding we suspend sound reasoning and head off into the unknown. Political warmongers use rhetoric that is designed to signify the "exceptional" nature of the situation and to transport the audience from the world of the "everyday" to the misty realm of the "**sacred**." This is, in part, the attractiveness of war: the suspension of the routine and the mundane and the transport to a world of inverted values and excitement, a world where egoism and market competition are replaced by self-sacrifice and cooperation among comrades (Fromm 1973: 135, 214). As Fromm indicates, troops do "not have to fight the members of his own group for food, medical care, shelter, clothing; these are all provided in a kind of perversely socialized system. The fact that war has these positive features is a sad comment on our civilization" (1973: 214–15). All that one has to do to enjoy this form of 'socialism' is to obey authority and be reduced to a tool.

DISCUSSION QUESTIONS

1. Is war a natural or a social phenomenon?
2. What are some of the rhetorical tricks that politicians and leaders use to manipulate their followers?
3. Can non-democratic institutions like the military be used to defend democracy?
4. Is a crisis situation the most rational moment to make important decisions that would send our fellow citizens into war?

VI: Conclusion

War and Freedom

Quite simply, war and democracy are incompatible. Every time the U.S. goes to war, we lose more of our freedoms and the balance of powers in the state concentrate rather than separate. War is too big a problem for one person to stop but, together, there are things we can do to stem the tide of death and destruction.

Justifications for War

The problem of war has preoccupied the minds of our most notable thinkers. For Aristotle, war was an unfortunate but necessary precondition for the enjoyment of peace (1988: 177); Thomas Aquinas thought that war was a "sin against peace" but justifiable insofar as the community was the victim of unprovoked aggression, the participants were authorized by the moral community, and violence was carried out with the intent to restore peace (Miller 2002); according to Rousseau, war was not a problem of relations between individuals or the enmity between a state and individuals or various and sundry groups but only in struggles over "property relations" between states ([1762] 1968: 56); for the German philosopher Hegel, war was an instrument that rulers used to periodically galvanize a population, thereby increasing the intensity and extent of social solidarity (1977: 272–73); for Marx and Engels, the whole history of human civilization (i.e., after primitive collective ownership gave way to private property) was "perpetual warfare, sometimes masked, sometimes open and acknowledged" between classes of oppressors and the oppressed (in Mills 1962: 46). But perhaps it was the philosopher Immanuel Kant who said it best:

> One must understand that the greatest evil that can oppress civilized peoples derives from *wars*, not, indeed, so much from actual present or past wars, as from the never-ending and constantly increasing *arming* for future war. To this all of the nation's powers are devoted, as are all those fruits of its culture that could be used to build a still greater culture; freedom will in many areas be largely destroyed, and the nation's motherly care for individual members will be changed into pitilessly hard demands that will be justified by concern over external dangers.
>
> (Kant 1983: 58)

We all have our own personal and ethical views on war. Pacifists condemn all forms of aggression and "realists" view the world as a kind of permanent clash of countervailing forces where one is most right where one has the most might and the real problem is simply a technical matter regarding how best to wage war. But as far as *absolute* ethical judgments go sustained analyses are unnecessary: War is either wholly wrong or wholly necessary—end of discussion; facts are piled up in defense of one position or another. But interpretive and critical schools of sociology, by contrast, view war as a problem *relative* to other social facts that require multidimensional analyses. This does not mean, however, that we forfeit our values or our obligation to arrive at a definite judgment. For example, from the standpoint of political sociology war represents a threat to democracy by distorting the balance of powers and concentrating decision-making in the hands of a few individuals. "Even when war is carefully considered, entered into as a last resort, and justified by external threats, it can still undermine the checks and balances, greatly empowering the executive while also making future wars more likely" (Jarecki 2008: 40). But determining that war is a threat to democracy means that we think democracy is good, that more democracy is better than less, and that democracy can be endangered both internally and externally.

War is not a natural phenomenon, but a social phenomenon. As such, a question like "Is war inevitable or somehow a permanent feature of human existence?" is missing the mark. It is true that as individuals the decision to initiate a war is typically not ours to make. Yet, some kinds of societies choose to pursue war whereas other types prefer peace. A "modest republic" may decide, time and again, to avoid entanglement in foreign adventures but a militarized state will find itself compelled repeatedly to engage in war. As Aristotle pointed out, "most … military states are safe only while they are at war, but fall when they have acquired their empire, like unused iron they lose their edge in time of peace" (1988: 178). For a nation with a massively overgrown military industrial complex (MIC) peace actually becomes a pathological condition to avoid at all costs. As it turns out, we do not enrich our military capacity to ensure peace but actually guarantee that through increased defense expenditures and militarization we shall never achieve peace. It seems that every time we think we are on the brink of one last war to end all wars (World War I) or a final victory over the enemy (e.g., the demise of the Soviet Union) another war is just around the corner.

The Permanence of War

At the beginning of this book I presented a definition of war that coincides fairly well with armed conflicts being carried out by discrete sovereign powers (e.g., a nation or state) punctuated by periods of relative peace: A picture of oscillation between war and peace, abnormality followed by a return to normality. As such, war retains its high degree of variability:

Warfare and preparation for warfare are often regarded as a nearly universal feature of human societies … however, it is … clear that the incidence of warfare is highly variable, and that in some societies there is little recourse to warfare and no tradition of militarism.

(Jary and Jary 1991: 548)

However, over the last generation or so a new picture is being drawn up in which war is emerging as a permanent feature of the global political system and becoming, unfortunately, the norm, with peace representing an abnormal condition. In short, wars waged between states followed by periods of peace are giving way, perhaps, to full-time armed conflict. At least three aspects need to be kept in mind as we move forward with analyses of war: First, the link between war and capitalism; second, the distribution of power within the federal government; and third, the emerging global imperial system.

War is business and it is profitable. In the early 1950s, General Douglas MacArthur summed up the situation well when he said: "'our country is now geared to an arms economy which was bred in an artificially induced psychosis of war hysteria and nurtured upon an incessant propaganda of fear'" (in Lens 1987: 42). What we learned in the aftermath of World War II is that mass destruction is great for corporate profits. Much of what we consider 'post-war prosperity' was predicated on the rebuilding of Europe and Japan from the 1940s into the 1960s and the Cold War with the Soviet Union. Even though the Cold War is over we have transferred the fear of communism to a fear of "Terror." As such, the essential linkage of capital and war and the arms industry remains intact. War is driven by corporate profits and corporations drive politics. What has melted away is the post-war welfare state and, in its place, the rise of the warfare state that has set aside the notion of "defense" for a very different idea of "security" (Hardt and Negri 2004: 21).

When we imagine "the government" we often conjure up an image of the president presiding over a vast system of highly coordinated control under his command ("the most powerful man in the world") or a balance of powers between the branches of government, each checking potential abuses on the part of the others. In reality "the government" is characterized by a dizzying array of power nodes and various currents sometimes reinforcing one another and sometimes clashing with countervailing power circuits. In other words, "the government" is actually in conflict with itself on a continuous basis. For example, the national security and intelligence apparatus, what Lens calls "the second government" (1987: 37), has routinely coordinated illegal wars and extra-legal activities (such as assassination attempts and coups) virtually unchecked by Congress.

So long as America acts as an empire then it will find itself embroiled in conflict.

Surrounded by colonial and dependent nations, underdeveloped, starving, and seething with unrest, the imperialist powers are continuously faced with challenges to their authority and to their dominance. The supply of potential incidents is thus more than ample, and opportunities for major or minor police actions offer themselves all the time. And these police actions create and recreate the danger of war, kindle and rekindle the fire under the boiling pot of mass hysteria.

(Baran 1957: 130)

Empire or imperial systems and wars are the poisons that will kill democracy.

War and Democracy

Beware the seduction of following warmongers who use the flowery rhetoric of "freedom," "democracy," and "liberation."

Leaders have all too frequently used the slogan that they are leading their people in a battle for freedom, when in reality their aim has been to enslave them. That no promise appeals more powerfully to the heart of man is evidences by the phenomenon that even those leaders who want to suppress freedom find it necessary to promise it.

(Fromm 1973: 199)

It is actually a testament to the American people that the Bush administration had to use propaganda, lies, and grand ideals like "freedom" and "liberty" in order to get the citizenry to consent to being dragged into war in the Middle East. People are not stupid but they can be manipulated. We must remember most of all that war and freedom are incompatible. If we value democracy and personal freedom then every war or 'police action' or whatever the government wants to call it, is a step further away from freedom and democracy. War is anti-democracy. War is anti-freedom. War is anti-liberty. Every single time the U.S. goes to war a little more public power is concentrated in the Executive branch of the federal government and the DoD creating an imbalance in our system of checks and balances. This has been going on since the 1940s when President Roosevelt used World War II to reorganize the state around a more powerful Executive and the "Executive is the branch of power most interested in war, and most prone to it" (Jarecki 2008: 26). Involvement in foreign war is the direct path to domestic tyranny (Jarecki 2008: 26). And we are currently well down that road.

As pure categories go, democracy and fascism are clearly distinct and very much opposed to one another. But outside the world of clear and distinct definitions, i.e., in the real world, democracy and fascism are not pure types or disconnected from one another—in other words, they are not diametrically opposed to one another but form a polarity. Polar opposites look as different as left and right, night and day, off and on, etc., but polar opposites always have "underground tunnels" and false bottoms and trap doors that lead from one polarity to another. Our democratic system of government is directly linked to its opposite, fascism, and many smart and serious thinkers are worried that we are either well on the road to becoming a fascist regime, if we are not a fascist regime already. It seems odd to even suspect that the home of the free and the land of the brave might be its exact opposite. But when we consider what is meant by "fascism" one begins to wonder.

Fascism is the harmonization or convergence of corporate power and the state combined with an expansionist and active military program. In other words: the fusion of capital, state, and war put us squarely in the domain of fascism. Now it is true that capital is the supreme power in the modern world but I do not think it is true, at least yet, that the state has been absolutely appropriated by capital. One can disagree: "We vote!" True, in a fascist regime voting either doesn't take place or is reduced to a farce (e.g., Cuba). But, then again, to what extent has voting in the U.S. been reduced to a farce? Take your pick of millionaire A or millionaire B. When President Obama was elected it seemed, for many, that "everything" had changed, that the status quo was at least temporarily turned upside down. But since Obama took office it has become obvious that in fact it is business as usual. Democrat or Republican, black or white, man or woman, Protestant or Catholic, etc., it makes little difference in how the state functions vis-à-vis capital and our reliance on war.

Breaking the Cycle of War

How do we stop war and strengthen our democratic institutions? Getting "acquainted" with or being "friendly" toward others is not enough to ward off aggression and collective violence "because [these attitudes and orientations] represent a superficial knowledge *about* another person, a knowledge of an "object" which I look at from the outside. This is quite different from the penetrating, empathic knowledge in which I understand the other's experiences by mobilizing those within myself which, if not the same, are similar to his" (Fromm 1973: 28). We need to recognize that we live in a single world now. Nation states may have outlived their usefulness. So long as we continue to think of ourselves as "Americans" first instead of human beings that need to coexist with all other human beings in a global human community, then we will continue down the road of war after war.

Aristotle's assessment of the Spartans may well apply, at least in part, to the U.S. and our penchant for war and materialism:

So long as they were at war ... their power was preserved, but when they had attained empire they fell, for the arts of peace they knew nothing, and have never engaged in any employment higher than war. There is another error, equally great, into which they have fallen. Although they truly think that the goods for which men contend are to be acquired by excellence rather than by vice, they err in supposing that these goods are to be preferred to the excellence which gains them.

(Aristotle 1988: 44)

In the introduction to this book I quoted Kant to the effect that the greatest evil challenging civilization and our hard-won freedoms is war. But Kant had more to say about war and his comments seem, at least on the surface, to contradict his earlier statement:

Yet, would there be even this culture, would there be the close connection among classes within the commonwealth deriving from their mutual economic well-being, would there be the large populations, indeed, would there even be the degree of freedom that still remains, even though severely limited by laws, if the constant fear of war did not necessitate this level of *respect for humanity* from the leaders of nations?

(Kant 1983: 58)

We might start to understand what Kant was getting at by expressing it as such: "You don't know what you have until you're about to lose it at the hands of an other." Kant was making a quite sophisticated argument about the origins of humanitarianism and the role of conflict and fear when it comes to identity formation. Fear of the dangerous other can bend the mind back upon itself such that, in its reflection, it discovers itself and values what it finds there. If there were no self to be found in the reflection there would also be no basis for a fear of death. Indeed, it is "self-esteem" that intensifies fear until it becomes terror. I cannot extend a veneration of the ego to another unless I possess it myself. As Durkheim indicates, it is none other than this *egoism* that serves as the basis for humanitarianism: "when [one] rates individual personality above all other ends, he respects it in others. His cult for it makes him suffer from all that minimizes it even among his fellows" (1951: 240). Our American egoism is our biggest defect if we wish to battle with groups willing to commit suicide to defeat us. A nation of egoists is unwilling to commit suicide to defeat the other. No technological advantage can trump the kind of self-sacrifice on tap in countries around the world that have reached the point where millions of people have nothing left to lose. The U.S. has not won an actual war since 1945; one defeat after another has plagued us: Korea, Vietnam, and now Afghanistan, the unwinnable quagmire. Why can the U.S. not win wars against nations that technologically lag behind us by decades or even centuries? Egoists employing fancy technology cannot defeat self-sacrifice taken to the point of death. But American egoism, if it is a defect for defeating our enemies, is also an asset in preventing war and building an international order that respects human life. As reflected in the quote by Kant above, I can only treat the other as a valuable self if I treat myself as valuable and irreplaceable. Love of the other is predicated on love of self.

Society continuously asks its members to sacrifice, to give something back, and to stop being selfish. Join the Army and belong to something bigger than yourself (i.e., be absorbed). If we want to stop war we need to be a bit more "selfish" and "individualistic" and stop throwing away our selves. Don't be a tool, in other words. The self as we know it has only been a late development reaching its apogee since the 16th century. The self, the individual, is the crowning achievement of human civilization; why throw it away? I'm not advocating narcissism or self-absorption—but rather rejecting the call of big transcendental commands and nebulous projects that promise to lift your little self up into something "larger" and more powerful. Recognizing that the state has orchestrated a set of structural problems that make the military life a "viable" alternative to school and work, the state will no longer be capable of waging wars if people simply stop participating. What else can be done?

Returning to a progressive tax structure that promotes greater equity in American life is one route to take by reinvesting in America—if we allow the rich and super-rich to enjoy unlimited wealth then we must also allow the rest of America to suffer unlimited misery; support progressive political candidates that promote a fair tax system—until then, find ways to "starve" the state by depriving it of avoidable funding; think outside the political "box" by voting for alternative party candidates or independents—the two big corporate parties are dead ends; buff up on propaganda techniques and tricks that politicians use to manipulate potential followers; be wary of politicians that use "tough talk" and populist rhetoric to lure voters away from progressive agendas—always remember that aesthetics plus politics equals death and destruction; following "charismatic" politicians is usually a dead end—listen to what the boring but rational voices are saying; war, capitalism, and defense spending are among our biggest social problems: Support politicians and activists that are focused on these issues; the traditional route to the world of work is not the only way: Exchange your time and skills with others in cooperative exchange systems; work toward alternative and cooperative communities; if you must "join" something, join the anti-war movement; when your government does or wants to do something stupid be sure and contact your representatives and get out of the house and march with others to protest; disobey; celebrate diversity and difference—so long as we stay trapped in conventional and traditional ways of thinking then we're trapped—ethnic minorities and people with different religions, sexual preferences, and "radical" politics are not your enemies; stay in school—an education is not just a utility to increase your wages, education is inherently a good thing; embrace internationalism; get your information from a variety of sources around the world; find ways to eliminate your use of fossil fuels; love the earth and your fellow human being, not abstract entities like nations and states; recycle and reuse when possible; buy used instead of new; barter instead of using cash; avoid going into debt; do not use credit cards to fuel your lifestyle; create your own culture instead of consuming prepackaged culture; limit consumption to needs not wants. Perhaps the single most important thing we can do resides in the direction of socialization of our children to reject violence, retaliation, punitive punishment, revenge, and the militarization of culture.

DISCUSSION QUESTIONS

1. Is there such a thing as a "good war"?
2. Is war compatible with democracy?
3. What are some things that can be done to eliminate war in the world?

References

Ali, Tariq. 2008. *The Duel*. New York: Scribner.

Alperovitz, Gar. 1996. *The Decision to Use the Atomic Bomb*. New York: Vintage.

Altemeyer, Bob. 1996. *The Authoritarian Specter*. Cambridge: Harvard University Press.

Amin, Samir. 1994. *Re-Reading the Postwar Period*. New York: Monthly Review Press.

Aristotle. 1988. *The Politics*. Cambridge: Cambridge University Press.

Baran, Paul A. 1957. *The Political Economy of Growth*. New York: Monthly Review Press.

Battle, Joyce (ed.). 2003. "Shaking Hands with Saddam Hussein: The US Tilts toward Iraq, 1980–84." National Security Archive Electronic Briefing Book No. 82, George Washington University. Retrieved June 11, 2010 (http://www.gwu.edu/~nsarchiv/NSAEBB/NSAEBB82/).

Braverman, Harry. 1974. *Labor and Monopoly Capital*. New York: Monthly Review Press.

Bremmer, Ian. 2010. *The End of the Free Market*. New York: Portfolio.

Caillois, Roger. 1959. *Man and the Sacred*, translated by Meyer Barash. Urbana and Chicago: University of Illinois Press.

Cassano, Graham. 2009. "Symbolic Exploitation and the Social Dialectic of Desire." *Critical Sociology, 35*(3): 379–93.

Chandrasekaran, Rajiv. 2006. *Imperial Life in the Emerald City*. New York: Alfred A. Knopf.

Chatterjee, Pratap. 2010. *Halliburton's Army*. New York: Nation Books.

Cleveland, William L., and Martin Bunton. 2009. *A History of the Modern Middle East*, fourth edition. Boulder, CO: Westview Press.

CNN. 2010. "Drone Crew Criticized in Afghan Strike." *CNN Online*, May 29. Retrieved May 29, 2010 (http://www.cnn.com/2010/WORLD/asiapcf/05/29/us.afghan.civilian.deaths).

Dolnick, Sam. 2010. "Kerik is Sentenced in Corruption Case." *New York Times*, February 18. Retrieved June 21, 2010 (http://www.nytimes.com/2010/02/19/nyregion/19kerik.html).

Durkheim, Emile. 1951. *Suicide*, translated by John A. Spaulding and George Simpson. New York: The Free Press.

———. 1995. *The Elementary Forms of Religious Life*, translated by Karen Fields. New York: Free Press.

Ellul, Jacques. 1965. *Propaganda*. New York: Vintage.

Fisk, Robert. 2009. "The Demise of the Dollar." *The Independent*, October 6. Retrieved June 26, 2010 (http://www.globalpolicy.org/globalization/globalization-of-the-economy-2-1/dollarization/48265.html).

Foster, John Bellamy, and Fred Magdoff. 2009. *The Great Financial Crisis*. New York: Monthly Review Press.

Frank, Andre Gunder. 1979. *Dependent Accumulation and Underdevelopment*. New York: Monthly Review Press.

Fromm, Erich. 1941. *Escape from Freedom*. New York: Henry Holt.

———. 1973. *The Anatomy of Human Destructiveness*. New York: Holt, Rinehart and Winston.

Gelvin, James L. 2008. *The Modern Middle East*, second edition. New York and Oxford: Oxford University Press.

Gramsci, Antonio. 1971. *Selections from the Prison Notebooks*. New York: International Publishers.

Greenwald, Robert. 2006. *Iraq for Sale*. Brave New Films.

Hamblin, William J. 2006. *Warfare in the Ancient Near East to 1600 BC*. New York: Routledge.

Hardt, Michael, and Antonio Negri. 2004. *Multitude*. New York: Penguin.

Harrison, Bennett and Barry Bluestone. 1988. *The Great U-Turn*. New York: Basic Books.

Harvey, David. 1990. *The Condition of Postmodernity*. Cambridge: Blackwell.

———. 2003. *The New Imperialism*. New York: Oxford University Press.

Hedges, Chris. 2002. *War is a Force that Gives Us Meaning*. New York: Anchor.

Hegel, G. W. F. 1956. *The Philosophy of History*, translated by J. Sibree. Mineola, New York: Dover.

———.1977. *Phenomenology of Spirit*, translated by A. V. Miller. Oxford: Oxford University Press.

Heidelberg Institute for International Conflict Research. 2009. *Conflict Barometer 2009*. Department of Political Science Heidelberg University.

Henig, Ruth. 1993. *The Origins of the First World War*, second edition. London and New York: Routledge.

Hoffman, David E. 2009. *The Dead Hand: The Untold Story of the Cold War Arms Race and Its Dangerous Legacy*. New York: Doubleday.

Iraq Family Health Survey Study Group. 2008. "Violence-Related Mortality in Iraq from 2002 to 2006." *The New England Journal of Medicine* 358(5): 484–93.

Isbister, John. 2001. *Promises not Kept*, fifth edition. Bloomfield, Connecticut: Kumarian Press.

Jarecki, Eugene. 2008. *The American Way of War*. New York: Free Press.

Jary, David, and Julia Jary (eds.). 1991. *The Harper Collins Dictionary of Sociology*. New York: Harper Perennial.

Johnson, Alvin. 1934. "War." Pp. 331–42 in *Encyclopaedia of the Social Sciences*, Vol. 15. New York: Macmillan.

Johnston, David Cay. 2007. "Income Gap is Widening, Data Says." *New York Times*, March 29. Retrieved June 16, 2010 (http://www.nytimes.com/2007/03/29/business/29tax.html).

Kant, Immanuel. 1983. *Perpetual Peace and Other Essays*. Indianapolis and Cambridge: Hackett Publishing Co.

Keen, Sam. 1986. *Faces of the Enemy*. New York: Harper and Row.

Krier, Dan. 2005. *Speculative Management*. Albany: State University of New York Press.

Lasswell, Harold D. 1971. *Propaganda Technique in World War I*. Cambridge: The MIT Press.

Leicht, Kevin T., and Scott T. Fitzgerald. 2007. *Postindustrial Peasants*. New York: Worth.

Lens, Sidney. 1987. *Permanent War*. New York: Schocken Books.

Mandel, Ernest. 1975. *Late Capitalism*, translated by Joris De Bres. London and New York: Verso.

Mannheim, Karl. 1936. *Ideology and Utopia*. New York: Harcourt, Brace and World.

Marx, Karl. 1976 [1867]. *Capital*, Vol. 1. New York: Vintage.

———. 1981 [1894]. *Capital*, Vol. 3. New York: Penguin.

Marx, Karl and Frederick Engels. 1977 [1848]. *Manifesto of the Communist Party*, second revised edition. Moscow: Progress Publishers.

Massing, Paul. 1949. *Rehearsal for Destruction*. New York: Harper.

Mayer, Jane. 2009. "The Predator War." *The New Yorker*, October 26. Retrieved May 24, 2010 (http://www.newyorker.com/reporting/2009/10/26/091026fa_fact_mayer).

Miller, Richard B. 2002. "Aquinas and the Presumption against Killing and War." *The Journal of Religion, 82*(2): 173–204.

Mills, C. Wright. 1956. *The Power Elite*. Oxford: Oxford University Press.

———. 1962. *The Marxists*. New York: Dell.

Muralidharan, Sukumar. 2003. "Reimposing the Dollar Hegemony." *Frontline* (India), April 26–May 9. Retrieved June 26, 2010 (http://www.globalpolicy.org/component/content/article/168/34768.html).

O'Connor, James. 1984. *Accumulation Crisis*. New York: Basil Blackwell.

Pollock, Friedrich. 1982 [1941]. "State Capitalism: Its Possibilities and Limitations." Pp. 71–94 in *The Essential Frankfurt School Reader*. New York: Continuum.

Rashid, Ahmed. 2000. *Taliban*. New Haven: Yale University Press.

———. 2009. *Descent into Chaos*. New York: Penguin.

Riechmann, Deb, and Anne Flaherty. 2010. "Huge Obstacles Seen in Exploiting Afghan Minerals." *Associated Press*, June 14. Retrieved June 15, 2010 (http://www.npr.org/templates/story/story.php?storyId=127825235).

Rousseau, Jean-Jacques. 1968 [1762]. *The Social Contract*. New York: Penguin.

Sayle, Murray. 1995. "Did the Bomb End the War?" *The New Yorker*, July 31: 40–64.

Schmitt, Carl. 1996 [1932]. *The Concept of the Political*, translated by George Schwab. Chicago and London: University of Chicago Press.

Slotkin, Richard. 1973. *Regeneration through Violence*. New York: Harper.

Smith, Michael K. 2001. *The Greatest Story Never Told*. Xlibris.

Taylor, Philip M. 1990. *Munitions of the Mind*. Wellingborough, England: Patrick Stephens Limited.

———. 1998. *War and the Media*, second edition. Manchester: Manchester University Press.

Tierney, John F. (Chair), Majority Staff of the Subcommittee on National Security and Foreign Affairs. 2010. *Warlord, Inc.: Extortion and Corruption Along the U.S. Supply Chain in Afghanistan*. Washington, DC: Committee on Oversight and Government Reform, U.S. House of Representatives. Retrieved 30 August 2010 (http://oversight.house.gov/index.php?option=com_content&task=view&id=4993&Itemid=30).

Tripp, Charles. 2007. *A History of Iraq*, third edition. Cambridge: Cambridge University Press.

Weber, Max. 1978. *Economy and Society*. Berkeley: University of California Press.

Wolf, Eric. 1982. *Europe and the People without History*. Berkeley: University of California Press.

Worrell, Mark P. 1999. "The Veil of Piacular Subjectivity: Buchananism and the New World Order." *Electronic Journal of Sociology*, 4(3). Retrieved June 16, 2010 (http://www.sociology.org/content/vol004.003/buchanan.html).

Zakaria, Fareed. 2010. "Terrorism's Supermarket." *Newsweek*, May 7. Retrieved June 30, 2010 (http://www.newsweek.com/2010/05/07/terrorism-s-supermarket.html).

Zizek, Slavoj. 2010. *Living in the End Times*. London and New York: Verso.

Glossary/Index

9/11 3, 11, 23, 45, 47

A

Abu Ghraib: the infamous prison in Iraq where photographic evidence of detainee torture, rape, and murder by U.S. military personnel and other civilian contractors was leaked to the media in 2004 16

Afghanistan 9–12
    civilian casualties 12–13
    drone attacks 12–14
    geo-strategic position 10–11
    monetary costs of U.S. war in 14
    natural resources 9–10
    pipelines through 36
    Soviet occupation 10
    US interest in 10, 11
    U.S. occupation of 11–12, 54
    U.S. troops wounded and killed in 12

al Qaeda: meaning 'the base,' as in a foundation or military base, al Qaeda is an Islamic fundamentalist terrorist organization operating in and around Pakistan 10, 11, 14

amateurism 17–18

American Dream 27

Amin, Samir 2

Aquinas, Thomas 49

Arab-Israeli War 1973 5

Aristotle 49, 50, 53–54

Asia
    challenge to hegemony of U.S. 9, 12, 32, 34, 37
    energy resources 36

atomic bomb in World War II 34–36

authoritarianism 38–39, 44

F

fascism: a political system in which corporate interests have taken over control of the government and use police and military coercion both internally and externally to further the interests of capital, business, and finance 21, 44, 52–53

fetishism: the belief that some object or course of action possesses magical powers. Lucky charms, dashboard icons, rituals, gambling, etc., are all fetish forms of conduct 30

First Gulf War 7, 41

Fitzgerald, Scott 22, 23, 30

Fordism 20–21

Fromm, Erich 42, 44, 46, 48, 52, 53

G

Gelvin, James 1, 4, 5, 7, 47

Germany 4, 9, 24

good vs. evil 31, 45–47

Gramsci, Antonio 21

H

Halliburton 15

Hardt, Michael 9, 18–19, 51

Harvey, David 8, 9, 21, 25, 29, 31, 32, 38, 43

Hedges, Chris 43, 45, 46

Hegel, G.W.F. 18, 49

hegemony: any kind of power that any social group (nation, status group, class, party) has over another group of whatever kind. This power can be economic, political, military, cultural, ideological, intellectual, etc. 3

challenge to U.S. 9, 12, 25, 32, 33, 34, 37

Heidelberg Institute for International Conflict Research 1–2

housing market collapse 28

humanitarianism 54

Hussein, Saddam 6, 7, 8, 9

hypercapitalism: practices such as speculation that go "beyond" what we associate with classical capitalism 37

I

ideology: a system of authoritative ideas that provides ready-made or preconceived explanations and justifications for the way reality is, how the world works, and how normal people should act, think, and feel 39, 43, 46

nationalism as 47

imperialism: the military, economic, and political domination of one nation over another nation or set of interconnected nations forming a system of inequality, exploitation, and servitude 3, 5

role in fate of Iraq 8, 9, 32

U.S. system of 8, 9, 25, 32, 33, 51–52

incomes

inequality of 29

stagnation of 22, 28, 30

India 10, 11, 12, 34, 35

instrumentalization of human life 30–31

International Monetary Fund (IMF) 8, 32

Iran

1953 coup 7–8

war with Iraq 6

Iraq 4–9

allies of 7

civilian casualties of U.S. war in 12

coalition of bankrupts in 32

control over oil in 3, 5–6, 8, 9, 32

exodus of middle classes from 17

invasion of Kuwait 7

monetary costs of U.S. war in 14

plan to denominate oil reserves in euros 32

private contractors working in 15–17

rebuilding of 8, 16–18

role of imperialism in deciding fate of 8, 9, 31

Soviet relationship with 5, 6

U.S. invasion of 1, 3, 9, 25, 26, 32, 35

U.S. troops wounded and killed in 12

war with Iran 6

Iraq Petroleum Company 5

Isbister, John 5–6

J

Japan 35–36

Johnston, David 29

journalism 40–41

K

Kant, Immanuel 49–50, 54–55

Keen, Sam 1, 46

monopolization: the exclusive control over production, distribution, or sale of commodities. There is a lack of competition and prices are set without regard for market dynamics. 20

Muralidharan, Sukumar 32
"mutually assured destruction" (MAD) 34

N
nationalism 28, 29, 47
Negri, Antonio 9, 18–19, 51
New England Journal of Medicine 12
New York Times 29
North Korea 9, 12
nuclear capability 34–36
    and juxtaposition with torture 19
    of Pakistan 12
nuclear winter: the envelopment of the planet in a thick cloud of dust and debris
    that, blocking out sufficient sunlight, leads to mass extinction of plant and animal
    life 34

O
Obama, Barack 13, 21, 53
obedience 46
oil
    in Central Asia 36
    in Iran 7
    in Iraq 3, 5–6, 8, 9, 32
Organization of the Petroleum Exporting Countries (OPEC) 5–6
Osama bin Laden: the leader of al Qaeda, the supposed mastermind behind the 11
    September 2001 terrorist attacks, and promoter of a theocratic form of Islamic
    government including the rule of sacred laws and holy war (jihad) against enemies
    of Islam
Ottoman Empire
    collapse of 3–4
    dividing up of 4–5

P
pacifism 50
Pakistan 10–13
Panetta, Leon 11
patriotism: conventionally defined as love of one's country. Dynamically, patriotism
    is defined by a hatred of people and societies that are different. 29, 46–47
polarization: in this sense, the pulling apart of a society in two opposite directions,
    e.g., the rich and the poor, owners and workers, etc. 16
    class 27

political spectacle 43

post-Fordism 22, 38

post-industrial economy 20–24

power elite: a small complex of key figures, e.g. financiers and bankers, corporate movers and shakers (especially key figures in the defense industry), top military brass, select elected officials, some high-level career bureaucrats, powerful opinion-shapers in the media, religious leaders and maybe even some celebrities. 9, 23, 27, 29, 37

praxis: the unity of conceptualization, experience, judgment, imagination, creative action, and emotion. Praxis is dismantled or undermined by the division of labor, in which complex tasks requiring skill are broken down such that 'anybody' could do them. 27

private contractors 14, 15–17

propaganda 40–41, 44–45, 46

R

Reagan, Ronald 22, 38

Rolling Stone 23

Roosevelt, Franklin D. 52

Rousseau, Jean-Jacques 49

Russia 4, 9, 10, 24

    challenge to U.S. hegemony 9, 12, 32, 34, 37

    interest in Afghanistan 11

    state capitalism 36, 37

S

sacred: there are two forms of the sacred: The sacred pure (good) and the sacred impure (evil). Both gods and devils, law-abiders and criminals, etc., are therefore equally sacred. 58

Schmitt, Carl 45

security and secrecy 38–40

self-destructiveness 43–44

Single Integrated Operational Plan (SIOP) 34

Smith, Michael 35–36

socialization for war 42–45

state capitalism 36–37

state security and secrecy 38–39

status group: a system of using symbols and identities to differentiate members of a society into higher and lower standings. For example, speaking English, being male, and white are all signs of higher social standing in the United States. 1

Suez Canal 7

Sullivan, Paul 12
symbolic compensations 28–29

T

taboo: more than simply moral prohibitions or "the forbidden"—a taboo object or
    action possesses some sinister and impure but also *alluring* moral power or capac-
    ity that fascinates the person afflicted by taboo forms of thought 29
Taliban: originally a movement of pious religious students (the name literally means
    "students") that rose to power and governed Afghanistan until their overthrow in
    2001, at which time they were converted into an insurgent group that operates in
    and around Pakistan attempting to regain lost ground against the U.S. 10, 11, 13
taxes 8, 22, 32, 55
Taylor, Philip 40, 41
Thatcher, Margaret 38
torture 18–19
Tripp, Charles 5, 6, 7

U

unemployment and underemployment 26, 42, 43
us vs. them 31, 45–47
USSR
    in Afghanistan 10
    in Cold War 21, 31, 34
    collapse of 34, 36
    message from U.S. in dropping of atomic bombs 35–36
    relationship with Iraq 5, 6

V

Veterans for Common Sense (VCS) 12
Vietnam 2, 35, 54
voting in U.S. 53

W

wage stagnation 22, 28, 30
war
    attractiveness of 48
    breaking cycle of 53–56
    defining 1
    and democracy 50, 52–53
    and extraordinary situations 47–48
    justifications for 49–50